Praise for
More About So Requirements: Thorny Issues and Practical Advice

"A must-have—Weigers goes well beyond aphorisms with practical insights for everyone involved in the requirements process. This book is an experience-based, insightful discussion of what the software requirements expert ought to know to get better at his or her job. It's the book you should read after whatever book you read to get an introduction to the topic of software requirements.

There's a whole lot of reality in this relatively small volume. There is a section on 'Managing Scope Creep,' and another on 'The Fuzzy Line Between Requirements and Design,' that are worth the price of the book just because of the light they shine on some particularly difficult issues. I like this book. Its author speaks with experience and authority, in a readable way, with lots of nice illuminating anecdotes."

—Robert L. Glass, Publisher/Editor, *The Software Practitioner*, **Visiting Professor, Griffith University, Australia**

"In an easy-to-read format, *More About Software Requirements* offers practical answers to the most vexing requirements problems faced by analysts and project managers. An essential companion to Wiegers's *Software Requirements*, it cuts to the chase with real-world wisdom for practitioners. Use this book to find the bottom-line advice you need to succeed with your requirements efforts."

—Ellen Gottesdiener, EBG Consulting; Author, *Requirements by Collaboration* **and** *Software Requirements Memory Jogger*

"Karl has done it again, he has captured the difficult requirement questions, provided sensible solutions, and shown us the related pitfalls.

If you do anything with software requirements you will find answers to your difficult questions clearly addressed and solution pros and cons plainly delineated."

—Ivy Hooks, Compliance Automation, Inc.

"Sage advice from a requirements master. And, fortunately, Wiegers is a great writer, too. Professionals who take requirements seriously—and we all should take requirements seriously—must read this book."

—Norm Kerth, Principal, Elite Systems

"If you have requirements problems (and who doesn't), this book will help. *More About Software Requirements* is filled with pragmatic down-to-earth advice. Wiegers helps the entire project team—project managers, developers, testers, and writers, not just the requirements analysts—understand what's happening with their requirements and how to fix those problems. Make this book required reading for your whole project team."

—Johanna Rothman, President of Rothman Consulting Group, Inc.; Coauthor, *Behind Closed Doors: Secrets of Great Management;* **Author,** *Hiring the Best Knowledge Workers, Techies & Nerds: The Secrets and Science of Hiring Technical People*

"Karl Wiegers has added to the treasure trove of advice in *Software Requirements, Second Edition,* by addressing some of the trickiest and most controversial issues in requirements engineering. I get asked questions in the areas covered in *More About Software Requirements* all the time.

The advice is sound; the writing is clear. This is a very useful, practical book."

—Erik Simmons, Requirements Engineering Program Lead, Corporate Quality Network, Intel Corporation

More About Software Requirements:
Thorny Issues and Practical Advice

Karl E. Wiegers

PUBLISHED BY
Microsoft Press
A Division of Microsoft Corporation
One Microsoft Way
Redmond, Washington 98052-6399

Library of Congress Control Number 2005936071

Printed and bound in the United States of America.

1 2 3 4 5 6 7 8 9   QWE   0 9 8 7 6 5

Distributed in Canada by H.B. Fenn and Company Ltd.

A CIP catalogue record for this book is available from the British Library.

Microsoft Press books are available through booksellers and distributors worldwide. For further information about international editions, contact your local Microsoft Corporation office or contact Microsoft Press International directly at fax (425) 936-7329. Visit our Web site at www.microsoft.com/mspress. Send comments to mspinput@microsoft.com.

Acquisitions Editor: Ben Ryan
Project Editor: Devon Musgrave
Copy Editor: Michelle Goodman
Indexer: Brenda Miller

Body Part No. X11-66734

Contents at a Glance

Table of Contents

Preface

Requirements engineering continues to be a hot topic in the software industry. More and more development organizations realize that they cannot succeed unless they get the software requirements right. Too often, the people responsible for leading the requirements process are ill-equipped for this challenging role. They do the best they can, but it's an uphill climb without adequate training, coaching, resources, and experience.

As a consultant, trainer, and author, I receive many questions from practitioners about how to handle difficult requirements issues. Certain questions come up over and over again. Alas, there aren't simple answers for many of these. Many books on requirements engineering have been published during the last several years, including my own, *Software Requirements, Second Edition* (Wiegers 2003a). These books provide solid guidance on the challenges of requirements elicitation, analysis, specification, validation, and management. However, additional requirements topics are not covered well by the existing books. Also, some books contain guidance that I believe is ill-founded.

This book addresses some of these recurrent questions that puzzle and frustrate requirements analysts, such as the following:

- "How do I keep too much design from being embedded in the requirements?" (I heard this question again the day before I wrote these words.)
- "When should I baseline my requirements?"
- "How can I convince my managers that we need to do a better job on our project requirements?"
- "What are some good questions to ask in requirements interviews?"
- "Are use cases all I need for documenting the requirements?"
- "We can't get our customers to review the requirements specification. What should I do?"
- "What are some good metrics our organization should collect about our requirements?"
- "We're collecting requirements for multiple releases concurrently. How should I store those?"
- "How can I use requirements to estimate how long it will take to finish the project?"
- "How can I write better requirements?"

I've addressed some other topics in this book simply because little has been written about them. For instance, everyone talks about project scope, but the current books on requirements engineering say little about how to actually define scope. See Chapter 17, "Defining Project Scope," for some recommendations. Still other topics are included because I don't see practitioners using some of the established techniques that can help them do a better job. As an example, nearly all requirements specifications I see consist entirely of written text—there's not a picture to be found. However, the skilled analyst should have a rich tool kit of techniques available for representing requirements information. Text is fine in many cases, but other sorts of requirements "views" sometimes are more valuable. Chapter 19, "The Six Blind Men and the Requirements," addresses this topic.

The suggestions I propose in this book augment the "good practices" approach I took in my earlier book. Many cross-references are provided to chapters in *Software Requirements, Second Edition*, marked with the icon shown to the left of this paragraph. As with all such advice, you need to think about how best to apply these suggestions to your specific situation. Organizations are different, projects are different, and cultures are different, so techniques that work in one situation might not be just right for another. To illustrate the application of these practices, I've included many examples of actual project experiences, marked with the "true stories" icon shown to the left here.

Anyone involved with defining or understanding the requirements for a new or enhanced software product will find this book useful. The primary audience consists of those team members who perform the role of the requirements analyst on a software development project, be this their full-time job or just something they do once in awhile. Part II of this book, "On the Management View of Requirements," is focused on aspects of requirements engineering that are of particular interest to project managers and senior managers. Customer representatives who work with the software team will also find certain chapters valuable, particularly those in Part III, "On Customer Interactions," and Part IV, "On Use Cases."

I should point out that all the practices I recommend assume that you're dealing with reasonable people. Sometimes an unreasonable customer will insist on a specific solution that isn't a good fit for the problem. Unreasonable funding sponsors might impose their own inappropriate preferences, overriding the thoughtful decisions made by actual user representatives. Senior managers or influential customers sometimes demand impossible delivery dates for an overly constrained project. If you face such a situation, try educating the difficult people to help them understand the risks posed by the approaches they are demanding and the value of using a better approach. People who appear unreasonable often are just uninformed. Sometimes, though, they truly are unreasonable. I can't help you much with that.

You may download the templates and other process assets described in this book from the Process Impact Web site, *http://www.processimpact.com*. Feel free to share your experiences with me at kwiegers@acm.org.

I hope you'll find this book a valuable supplement to your other resources for software requirements engineering. But don't just read the chapters and say, "That's interesting." Set yourself a personal goal of finding at least three new practices that you want to try the next few times you wear your analyst hat.

Acknowledgments

First, I thank the many people in my seminars who have asked some of these challenging questions over the past several years, as well as the readers who have sent me e-mails with their own thorny requirements issues. I'm grateful for the review input provided by Wayne Allen, Michael Beshears, Steven Davis, Chris Fahlbusch, Lynda Fleming, Betty Luedke, Jeannine McConnell, Terry Nooyen-Coyner, Debbie Shyne, David Standerford, Donna Swaim, and Robin Tucker. The many comments I received from reviewers Ellen Gottesdiener, Andre Gous, and Shannon Jackson were especially valuable. A special thanks goes to Erik Simmons, who provided incisive suggestions on every chapter and greatly helped me sharpen the message. Thanks also to the Microsoft Learning editorial and production teams, including acquisitions editor Ben Ryan, copy editor Michelle Goodman, proofreaders Becka McKay and Sandi Resnick, and artist Joel Panchot. I especially enjoyed the opportunity to work with project editor Devon Musgrave again.

And finally, a big thank-you once again to my ever-cheerful wife, Chris Zambito. Fooled you this time, hon!

Part I
On Essential Requirements Concepts

This book begins with an overview of some fundamental concepts and principles about software requirements engineering. One of the big obstacles that requirements analysts and other practitioners run into is a lack of common understanding of what "requirements" are and what the requirements engineering process entails. Chapter 1, "Requirements Engineering Overview," provides readers with a set of requirements-related terms that I'll use throughout the rest of the book. This should provide a sufficient foundation for understanding the subsequent chapters. For more details on any topic, please refer to *Software Requirements, Second Edition*.

Chapter 2, "Cosmic Truths About Software Requirements," presents several important insights about software requirements that every manager and practitioner should know. These truths apply to virtually every software project and software development organization, regardless of the nature of the product or the development methodologies being used. No matter what your role is on a project, keep these cosmic truths in mind anytime you're involved with requirements activities.

Chapter 1
Requirements Engineering Overview

Requirements engineering is one of the most challenging aspects of software development. It is also arguably the most important aspect, as it lays the foundation for all the subsequent project work. The past several years have seen a surge of interest in software requirements. People in many development organizations have elected to pursue better requirements practices because the pain from their current approaches has become too great. Many requirements analysts—those team members who coordinate the project's requirements engineering activities—also are enhancing their skills.

 This book does not cover the entire domain of software requirements engineering. Instead, I focus on selected topics that are chronic areas of difficulty and confusion for practitioners. Many excellent books on the requirements process are available. My own *Software Requirements, Second Edition* provides a solid tutorial. This introductory chapter provides some requirements definitions and principles adapted from my earlier book so that you'll have a conceptual foundation for understanding the rest of this book.

"Requirement" Defined

Here is my favorite definition of *requirement* (Sommerville and Sawyer 1997):

> *Requirements are...a specification of what should be implemented. They are descriptions of how the system should behave, or of a system property or attribute. They may be a constraint on the development process of the system.*

I like this definition because it points out that there are many kinds of information that fit into this big pot of soup we call "The Requirements." According to this definition, requirements describe what we're going to have when we're done with a project. "Descriptions of how the system should behave" refer to the functional requirements, the behaviors the system[1] will exhibit under various circumstances. Project participants naturally focus on functionality because that's what we observe when we use a product.

But requirements might also be descriptions of system properties, or attributes. Attributes describe not what the system does, but how well the system does its job. You've probably used some application that did exactly what it was supposed to do—but you hated it. Perhaps it was too clumsy to use or it didn't map to your business processes very well. Or maybe the application crashed a lot or it didn't interface well with other applications. These are examples of software that perhaps satisfied its functional requirements but did not satisfy the user's expectations of quality.

Other types of requirements might impose constraints on the development process, limits within which the developers must operate. Technology limitations (languages, platforms, database components) and user interface standards are two classes of constraints. So despite the natural emphasis on functionality, there's more to the requirements discussion.

Different Types of Requirements

The terminology used when discussing software requirements causes all sorts of confusion. Ten people who read a single requirement statement might each call it something different. They might term it a *business requirement, user requirement, system requirement, functional requirement, software requirement, product requirement, technical requirement, constraint, feature,* or simply a *requirement.*

To help address the requirements Tower of Babel, I've developed a simple model and a set of definitions for various types of requirements information (Wiegers 2003a). Figure 1-1 illustrates a way to think about the diverse types of requirements. As statistician George Box observed, "All models are wrong, but some models are useful." This saying applies here. The model is clearly a simplification (which is both a strength and a weakness of models), but I find it to be a helpful organizing scheme. Note that this model just represents product requirements. It doesn't cover nontechnical project requirements such as staffing, scheduling, communication, training, operational, and support issues.

The ovals in the figure represent types of requirements information. The rectangles indicate documents—containers, really—in which to store that information. These containers hold different types of information developed at different stages of the project based on input from different sources. The containers need not be separate documents or even traditional documents. They can be spreadsheets, index cards, or databases. It makes no sense to generate a plethora of documents on a small project, so you might choose to combine different types of requirements information in a single document.

---

1. I will use the terms "product," "system," and "application" interchangeably to refer to whatever software or software-containing deliverable your project is expected to produce.

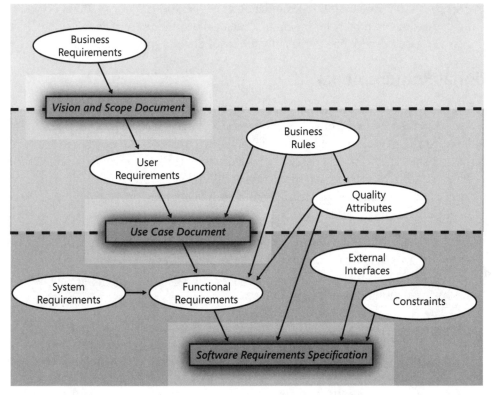

Figure 1-1   Connections among several types of requirements information.

I think in terms of three levels of software requirements: business requirements, user requirements, and functional requirements. In addition, the analyst must contend with various types of nonfunctional requirements and other associated information. These include business rules, quality attributes, external interface requirements, and design and implementation constraints.

Business Requirements

Business requirements represent a kind of "why" information. Business requirements describe why the organization is undertaking the project. They state some benefits that the developing organization or its customers expect to receive from the product. I like to record business requirements in a vision and scope document. Some organizations create a project charter, business case, or marketing requirements document for this purpose.

User Requirements

User requirements constitute one type of "what" information. User requirements describe what the user will be able to do with the product, such as goals or tasks that users must be able to perform. Use cases, scenarios, user stories, and event-response tables are some ways to represent user requirements (Alexander and Maiden 2004; Wiegers 2003a). If you're developing use cases, you might store them in a use case document. Some analysts prefer to include their use case descriptions in the software requirements specification (SRS).

Functional Requirements

Functional requirements represent another kind of "what" information. They describe what the developer is supposed to build. Sometimes called *behavioral requirements,* these are the traditional "shall" statements that describe what the system "shall do" or what the system "shall let the user do." The functional requirements and various other types of requirements information find a home in the software requirements specification. The SRS is the principal deliverable that analysts use to communicate detailed requirements information to developers, testers, and other project stakeholders.

In Figure 1-1, the fact that the arrows between these three requirement levels align from upper left to lower right is significant. Specifying the correct set of functionality to build into the product enables users to accomplish their tasks or to achieve their goals, thereby satisfying the business requirements.

System Requirements

In this context, system requirements don't mean the requirements for any old information system. I use the term *system requirements* (or *product requirements*) to describe the top-level requirements for a product that contains multiple subsystems. The requirements analyst might derive certain functional requirements directly from an understanding of the high-level requirements for the system as a whole. A system could contain only software components, or it could incorporate both software and hardware subsystems. People are a part of a system, too, so certain system functions might be allocated to human beings. Software requirements, then, represent the portion of a system's functional and nonfunctional requirements that are allocated to software components of the system.

A good example of a system in this sense is a cashier's workstation at a supermarket. The workstation includes a bar code scanner, often integrated with a scale. It has a keyboard and one or two displays. There's a card reader for customer credit or debit cards, and often a change dispenser is included. I've seen as many as three printers for customer sales receipts, credit card charge slips, and coupons. These components interact with each other, and each component implements a particular subset of the whole system's functionality.

People sometimes describe system requirements in the form of product features. I define a *feature* as a set of logically related functional requirements that provides a capability to the user and enables the satisfaction of a business objective (Wiegers 2003a). Exploring features is a very different perspective from considering user requirements based on user goals. Ideally, the features built into a product will be exactly those that let users perform their known and anticipated activities with the product. Sometimes, though, features are included in a commercial product because of perceived marketplace or competitive demands, not just because of expected usage patterns.

Business Rules

Business rules include corporate policies, government regulations, industry standards (such as accounting practices), and computational algorithms. Business rules are not themselves software requirements. They typically have an existence outside the boundaries of any specific software system and therefore should be regarded as an enterprise-level asset. However, business rules often require that specific functionality be implemented to ensure that the system enforces or complies with those rules. Business rules might restrict who can perform certain use cases, and they can influence quality attributes, such as security. Some business rules might be used to control internal system processing based on specific combinations of data values, system states, conditions, or other user-defined criteria. You can trace the origin of certain functional requirements back to the particular business rule from which it was derived.

Quality Attributes

Quality attributes describe the product's characteristics in various dimensions that are important either to users or to developers and maintainers. These characteristics include availability, performance, usability, portability, integrity, efficiency, robustness, and many others (Lauesen 2002). (See Chapter 12 of *Software Requirements, Second Edition.*) Sometimes these characteristics are called *quality factors* or *quality of service requirements*.

External Interfaces

External interfaces between the system and the outside world constitute another class of non-functional requirements. These encompass interfaces to other software components, to hardware devices, and to human users, as well as communications interfaces and protocols used to exchange information with other systems.

Constraints

Finally, we have design and implementation *constraints*, which are restrictions imposed on the choices available to the developer for some legitimate reason. Some people consider all requirements to be constraints, but this broad generalization isn't very helpful.

Requirements Engineering Activities

I find it useful to split the entire domain of software requirements engineering into *requirements development* and *requirements management*. The goal of requirements development is to identify, agree upon, and record a set of functional requirements and product characteristics that will achieve the stated business objectives. The central purpose of requirements management is to manage changes to a set of agreed-upon requirements that have been committed to a specific product release. Requirements management also includes tracking the status of individual requirements and tracing requirements both backward to their origins and forward into design elements, code modules, and tests.

Note that I'm not implying that projects should follow the classic waterfall or sequential life-cycle approach. You don't need to develop *all* the requirements for the entire product before you begin designing and constructing it. In fact, attempting to perfect a complete and stable set of requirements is an invitation to scope bloat and analysis paralysis. It ignores the reality that needs, concepts, and understanding will change as time passes and the product evolves. But whether you're specifying 1 percent or 100 percent of the ultimate product for a given release cycle, the team must understand the requirements for that portion before they can build it.

We can further subdivide requirements development into elicitation, analysis, specification, and validation, as illustrated in Figure 1-2 (Abran and Moore 2001). *Elicitation* involves the actions we go through to understand our users and discover their needs. A major requirements *analysis* activity is to derive more detailed requirements from higher-level requirements. Analysis also involves creating multiple views of the requirements, such as prototypes, graphical analysis models, and tests. Other aspects of requirements analysis include negotiating priorities, searching for missing requirements, and evaluating technical feasibility, risk, and failure modes. Analysis provides a feedback loop that refines the understanding that the analyst developed during an elicitation activity.

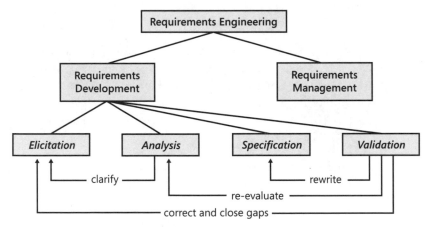

Figure 1-2   Subcomponents of requirements engineering.

Specification involves recording the various types of requirements information in forms that will facilitate communication among the project stakeholders. Traditionally these forms are documents containing natural language text. As we'll see in this book, though, other representation techniques also are valuable, such as graphical analysis models, tables, and mathematical expressions. The "specification" could consist of requirements information stored in a database, as in a commercial requirements management tool, rather than being a traditional document.

Finally, *validation* ensures that those requirements are correct, will satisfy customer needs, and have all the characteristics of high-quality requirements. Validation might lead the analyst to rewrite some requirements specifications, to reassess the initial analysis, or to correct and refine the set of documented requirements.

Iteration is the key to success in requirements development. Don't expect to take a single pass through elicitation, analysis, specification, and validation. You have to plan on multiple cycles, progressively refining the requirements to a suitable level of detail. When working as an analyst, I might talk to some users to get some information, analyze it, and check back with the users to clarify anything I didn't understand. Then I might write up what I've learned and pass that fragment of a specification to my user representatives for a quick, informal review. This process results in multiple elicitation cycles interleaved with quick review cycles. This iterative process is a way to accumulate higher-quality information, filter out misunderstandings, and add completeness a layer at a time. Note that the analyst could be performing elicitation, analysis, specification, and validation activities concurrently on different sets of requirements.

Requirements management commences when the team says they believe their requirements are good enough to serve as the foundation for design and construction of some portion of the product. At this point, the analyst defines a requirements *baseline*, a snapshot in time that represents the current reviewed, agreed-upon, and approved set of requirements for a specific product release. Project stakeholders make schedule and cost commitments based on the requirements baseline. Because changes in the baseline can affect those commitments, formal change control begins at the time the baseline is established.

Looking Ahead

Now that you've had this brief introduction to requirements engineering, you're ready to plunge into the rest of the book. Chapter 2, "Cosmic Truths About Software Requirements," describes several facts about requirements that apply to virtually all software projects. Part II of this book, "On the Management View of Requirements," presents several topics that will be of particular interest to software managers, including how to assess the business impact that requirements have on projects. The chapters in Part III, "On Customer Interactions," address several aspects of the critical involvement of customer representatives in the requirements process. Part IV, "On Use Cases," addresses some of the issues that trip up many development teams when they first try to apply this powerful technique for eliciting user requirements.

I recently received an e-mail from someone who had read my books and articles. He said, "But I still don't understand how to actually *write* the requirements." Unfortunately, there's no formulaic technique for writing requirements, just as there's no simple formula for writing anything else. It takes knowledge of the relevant information, practice, feedback on what you've written, and a solid understanding of what both good and bad requirements look like. Part V, "On Writing Requirements," presents much practical guidance on the topic of actually documenting good software requirements. Part VI, "On the Requirements Process," addresses the topics of defining project scope, establishing requirements baselines, and creating alternative requirements views. Finally, Part VII, "On Managing Requirements," wraps up with several chapters on the care and feeding of your requirements collections.

As you read these chapters, you'll get many ideas about how to do a better job of developing and managing the requirements for your next project. Always keep in mind the overarching goal of requirements engineering: clear and effective communication among the project stakeholders.

Chapter 2
Cosmic Truths About Software Requirements

In this chapter:

As every consultant knows, the correct answer to nearly any question regarding software is, "It depends." This isn't just a consultant's cop-out—it's true. The best advice for how to proceed in a given situation depends on the nature of the project, its constraints, the culture of the organization and team, the business environment, and other factors. But having worked with many organizations, I've made some observations about software requirements that really do seem to be universally applicable. This chapter presents some of these "cosmic truths" and their implications for the practicing requirements analyst.

Requirements Realities

Cosmic Truth #1: If you don't get the requirements right, it doesn't matter how well you execute the rest of the project.

Requirements are the foundation for all the project work that follows. I don't mean the initial SRS you come up with early in the project, but rather the full set of requirements knowledge that is developed incrementally during the course of the project.

The purpose of a software development project is to build a product that provides value to a particular set of customers. Requirements development attempts to determine the mix of product capabilities and characteristics that will best deliver this customer value. This understanding evolves over time as customers provide feedback on the early work and refine their expectations and needs. If this set of expectations isn't adequately explored and crafted into a set of product features and attributes, the chance of satisfying customer needs is slim.

As mentioned in the previous chapter, requirements validation is one of the vital subcomponents of requirements development, along with elicitation, analysis, and specification. Validation involves demonstrating that the specified requirements will meet customer needs. One useful technique for validating requirements is to work with suitable customer representatives to develop *user acceptance criteria*. These criteria define how customers determine whether they're willing to pay for the product or to begin using it to do their work. User acceptance criteria typically stipulate that the product allows the users to properly perform their most significant tasks, handles the common error conditions, and satisfies the users' quality expectations. User acceptance criteria aren't a substitute for thorough system testing. They do, however, provide a necessary perspective to determine whether the requirements are indeed right.

Cosmic Truth #2: Requirements development is a discovery and invention process, not just a collection process.

People often talk about "gathering requirements." This phrase suggests that the requirements are just lying around waiting to be picked like flowers or to be sucked out of the users' brains by the analyst. I prefer the term *requirements elicitation* to *requirements gathering*. Elicitation includes some discovery and some invention, as well as recording those bits of requirements information that customer representatives and subject matter experts offer to the analyst. Elicitation demands iteration. The participants in an elicitation discussion won't think of everything they'll need up front, and their thinking will change as the project continues. Requirements development is an exploratory activity.

The analyst is not simply a scribe who records what customers say. The analyst is an investigator who asks questions that stimulate the customers' thinking, seeking to uncover hidden information and generate new ideas. (See Chapter 7, "An Inquiry, Not an Inquisition.") It's fine for an analyst to propose requirements that might meet customer needs, provided that customers agree that those requirements add value before they go into the product (Robertson 2002). An analyst might ask a customer, "Would it be helpful if the system could do <whatever idea he has>?" The customer might reply, "No, that wouldn't do much for us." Or the customer might reply, "You could do that? Wow, that would be great! We didn't even think to ask for that feature, but if you could build it in, it would save our users a lot of time." This creativity is part of the value that the analyst adds to the requirements conversation. Just be careful that analysts and developers don't attempt to define a product from the bottom up through suggested product features, rather than basing the requirements on an understanding of stakeholder goals and a broad definition of success.

Cosmic Truth #3: Change happens.

It's inevitable that requirements will change. Business needs evolve, new users or markets are identified, business rules and government regulations are revised, and operating environments change over time. In addition, the business need becomes clearer as the key stakeholders become better educated about what their true needs are.

The objective of a change control process is not to inhibit change. Rather, the objective is to *manage* change to ensure that the project incorporates the right changes for the right reasons. You need to anticipate and accommodate changes to produce the minimum disruption and cost to the project and its stakeholders. However, excessive churning of the requirements after they've been agreed upon suggests that elicitation was incomplete or ineffective—or that agreement was premature. (See Chapter 18, "The Line in the Sand.")

To help make change happen, establish a change control process. You can download a sample from my Web site, *http://www.processimpact.com/goodies.shtml*. When I helped to implement a change control process in an Internet development group at Eastman Kodak Company, the team members properly viewed it as a structure, not as a barrier (Wiegers 1999). The group found this process invaluable for dealing with its mammoth backlog of change requests.

Every project team also needs to determine who will be evaluating requested changes and making decisions to approve or reject them. This group is typically called the change (or configuration) control board, or CCB. A CCB should write a charter that defines its composition, scope of authority, operating procedures, and decision-making process. A template for such a charter is available from *http://www.processimpact.com/goodies.shtml*.

Nearly every software project becomes larger than originally anticipated, so expect your requirements to grow over time. According to consultant Capers Jones (2000), requirements growth typically averages 1 to 3 percent per month during design and coding. This can have a significant impact on a long-term project. To accommodate some expected growth, build contingency buffers—also known as management reserve—into your project schedules (Wiegers 2002b). These buffers will keep your commitments from being thrown into disarray with the first change that comes along.

I once spoke with a manager on a five-year project regarding requirements growth. I pointed out that, at an average growth rate of 2 percent per month, his project was likely to be more than double the originally estimated size by the end of the planned 60-month schedule. The manager agreed that this was a possibility. When I asked if his plans anticipated this growth potential, he gave the answer I expected: No. I'm highly skeptical that this project will be completed without enormous cost and schedule overruns.

When you know that requirements are uncertain and likely to change, use an incremental or iterative development life cycle. Don't attempt to get all the requirements "right" up front and freeze them. Instead, specify and *baseline* the first set of requirements based on what is known at the time. A baseline is a statement about the state of the requirements at a specific point in time, such as "We believe that these requirements will meet customer needs and are a suitable foundation for proceeding with design and construction." Then implement that fraction of the product, get some customer feedback, and move on to the next slice of functionality. This is the intent behind agile development methodologies, the spiral model, iterative prototyping, evolutionary delivery, and other incremental approaches to software development.

Finally, recognize that change always has a price. Even the act of reviewing a proposed change and rejecting it consumes time. Software people need to educate their project stakeholders so they understand that, sure, we can make that change you just requested, and here's what it's going to cost. Then the stakeholders can make appropriate business decisions about which desired changes should be incorporated and at what time.

Requirements Stakeholders

Cosmic Truth #4: The interests of all the project stakeholders intersect in the requirements process.

Consultant Tim Lister once defined project success as "meeting the set of all requirements and constraints held as expectations by key stakeholders." A *stakeholder* is an individual or group who is actively involved in the project, who is affected by the project, or who can influence its outcome. Figure 2-1 identifies some typical software project stakeholder groups. Certain stakeholders are internal to the project team, such as the project manager, developers, testers, and requirements analysts. Others are external, including customers who select, specify, or fund products; users who employ the systems; compliance certifiers; auditors; and marketing, manufacturing, sales, and support groups. The requirements analyst has a central communication role, being responsible for interacting with all these stakeholders. Further, the analyst is responsible for seeing that the system being defined will be fit for use by all stakeholders, perhaps working with a system architect to achieve this goal.

Figure 2-1   Some typical software project stakeholders.

At the beginning of your project, identify your key stakeholder groups and determine which individuals will represent the interests of each group. You can count on stakeholders having conflicting interests that must be reconciled. They can't all have veto power over each other. You need to identify early on the decision makers who will resolve these conflicts, and these decision makers must determine what their decision-making process will be. As my colleague Christian Fahlbusch, a seasoned project manager, points out, "I have found that there is usually one primary decision maker on a project, oftentimes the key sponsor within the organization. I don't rest until I have identified that person, and then I make sure he is always aware of the project's progress."

Cosmic Truth #5: Customer involvement is the most critical contributor to software quality.

Various studies have confirmed that inadequate customer involvement is a leading cause of the failure of software projects. Customers often claim they can't spend time working on requirements. However, customers who aren't happy because the delivered product missed the mark always find plenty of time to point out the problems. The development team is going to get the customer input it needs eventually. It's a lot cheaper—and a lot less painful—to get that input early on, rather than after the project is ostensibly done.

Customer involvement requires more than a workshop or two early in the project. Ongoing engagement by suitably empowered and enthusiastic customer representatives is a critical success factor for software development. Following are some good practices for engaging customers in requirements development:

- **Identify user classes.** Customers are a subset of stakeholders, and users are a subset of customers. You can further subdivide your user community into multiple *user classes* that have largely distinct needs (Gause and Lawrence 1999). Unrepresented user classes are likely to be disappointed with the project outcome.

- **Select product champions.** You need to determine who will be the literal voice of the customer for each user class. I call these people *product champions*. Ideally, product champions are actual users who represent their user-class peers. See Chapter 6, "The Myth of the On-Site Customer," for more about product champions.

- **Build prototypes.** Prototypes provide opportunities for user representatives to interact with a simulation or portion of the ultimate system. (See Chapter 13 of *Software Requirements, Second Edition*.) Prototypes are far more tangible than written requirements specifications. However, prototypes aren't a substitute for documenting the detailed requirements.

- **Agree on customer rights and responsibilities.** People who must work together rarely discuss the nature of their collaboration. The analyst should negotiate with the customer representatives early in the project to agree on the responsibilities each party has with respect to the requirements process. An agreed-upon collaboration strategy is a strong contributor to the participants' mutual success. See Chapter 2 of *Software Requirements, Second Edition* for some suggestions of customer rights and responsibilities in the requirements process.

Cosmic Truth #6: The customer is not always right, but the customer always has a point.

It's popular in some circles to do whatever any customer demands, claiming "The customer is always right." Of course, the customer is *not* always right! Sometimes customers are in a bad mood, uninformed, or unreasonable. If you receive conflicting input from multiple customers, which one of those customers is "always right"?

The customer may not always be right, but the analyst needs to understand and respect whatever point each customer is trying to make through his request for certain product features or attributes. The analyst needs to be alert for situations in which the customer could be in the wrong. Rather than simply promising anything a customer requests, strive to understand the rationale behind the customer's thinking and negotiate an acceptable outcome. Following are some examples of situations in which a customer might not be right:

- Presenting solutions in the guise of requirements.

- Failing to prioritize requirements or expecting the loudest voice to get top priority.

- Not communicating business rules and other constraints, or trying to get around them.

- Expecting a new software system to drive business-process changes.

- Not supplying appropriate representative users to participate in requirements elicitation.

- Failing to make decisions when analysts or developers need issues resolved.

- Not accepting the need for tradeoffs in both functional and nonfunctional requirements.

- Demanding impossible commitments.

- Not accepting the cost of change.

Requirements Specifications

Cosmic Truth #7: The first question an analyst should ask about a proposed new requirement is, "Is this requirement in scope?"

Anyone who's been in the software business for long has worked on a project that has suffered from scope creep. It is normal and often beneficial for requirements to grow over the course of a project. Scope creep, though, refers to the uncontrolled and continuous increase in requirements that makes it impossible to deliver a product on schedule.

To control scope creep, you need to have the project stakeholders agree on a scope definition, a boundary between the desired capabilities that lie within the scope for a given product release and those that do not. (See Chapter 17, "Defining Project Scope," for some scope-definition techniques.) Then, whenever some stakeholder proposes a new functional requirement, feature, or use case, the analyst can ask, "Is this in scope?" To help answer this question, some project teams write their scope definition on a large piece of cardstock, laminate it, and bring it to their requirements elicitation discussions.

If a specific requirement is deemed out of scope one week, in scope the next, then out of scope again later, the project's scope boundary is not clearly defined. And that's an open invitation to scope creep.

Cosmic Truth #8: Even the best requirements document cannot—and should not—replace human dialogue.

Even the best requirements specification won't contain every bit of information the developers and testers need to do their jobs. There will always be tacit knowledge that the stakeholders assume (rightly or wrongly) that other participants already know, along with the explicit knowledge that must be documented in the SRS. Analysts and developers will always need to talk with knowledgeable users and subject matter experts to refine details, clarify ambiguities, and fill in the blanks. This is the rationale behind having some key customers, such as product champions, work intimately with the analysts and developers throughout the project. The person performing the role of requirements analyst (even if this is one of the developers) should coordinate these discussions to make sure that all the participants reach the same understanding so that the pieces all fit together properly. A written specification is still valuable and necessary, though. A documented record of what stakeholders agreed to at a point in time is more reliable than human memory.

You need more detail in the requirements specifications if you aren't going to have opportunities for frequent conversations with user representatives and other decision makers. (See Chapter 13, "How Much Detail Do You Need?") A good example of this is when you're outsourcing the implementation of a requirements specification that your team created. Expect to spend considerable time on review cycles to clarify and agree on what the requirements mean. Also expect delays in getting questions answered and decisions made, which can slow down the entire project. This very issue was a major contributing factor in a lawsuit I know of between a software package vendor and a customer (Wiegers 2003b). The vendor allowed no time in the schedule for review following some requirements elicitation workshops, planning instead to begin construction immediately. Months later, many key requirements issues had not yet been resolved and the actual project status didn't remotely resemble the project plan.

Cosmic Truth #9: The requirements might be vague, but the product will be specific.

Specifying requirements precisely is hard! You're inventing something new, and no one is exactly sure what the product should be and do. People sometimes are comfortable with vague requirements. Customers might like them because it means they can redefine those requirements later on to mean whatever they want them to mean at any given moment. Developers sometimes favor vague requirements because they allow the developers to build whatever they want to build. This is all great fun, but it doesn't lead to high-quality software.

Ultimately, you are building only one product, and someone needs to decide just what that product will be. If customers and analysts don't make the decisions, the developers will be forced to. This is a sign that the key stakeholders are abdicating their responsibility to make requirements-level decisions, leaving those decisions to people who know far less about the problem.

Don't use uncertainty as an excuse for lack of precision. Acknowledge the uncertainty and find ways to address it, such as through prototyping. A valuable adjunct to simply specifying each requirement is to define *fit criteria* that a user or tester could employ to judge whether the requirement was implemented correctly and as intended (Robertson and Robertson 1999). Attempting to write such fit criteria will quickly reveal whether a requirement is stated precisely enough to be verifiable.

Cosmic Truth #10: You're never going to have perfect requirements.

Requirements are never finished or complete. There is no way to know for certain that you haven't overlooked some requirement, and there will always be some requirements that the analyst won't feel it is necessary to record. Rather than declaring the requirements "done" at some point, define a baseline. (See Chapter 18.) Once you've established a baseline, follow your change control process to modify the requirements, recognizing the implications of making changes. It's folly to think you can freeze the requirements and allow no changes after some initial elicitation activities.

Striving for perfection can lead to analysis paralysis. Analysis paralysis, in turn, can have a backlash effect. Stakeholders who have been burned once by a project that got mired in requirements issues are reluctant to invest in requirements development on their next project.

You don't succeed in business by writing a perfect SRS. From a pragmatic perspective, requirements development strives for requirements that are *good enough* to allow the team to proceed with design, construction, and testing at an acceptable level of risk. The risk is the threat of having to do expensive and unnecessary rework. Have team members who will need to base their own work on the requirements review them to judge whether they provide a suitably solid foundation for that subsequent work. Keep this practical goal of "good enough" in mind as you pursue your quest for quality requirements.

Part II
On the Management View of Requirements

Project managers are vital stakeholders in the requirements process. Senior managers also are affected by requirements issues for the projects their organizations undertake. The three chapters in Part II provide some perspectives on requirements that will be of particular interest to managers at various levels.

Chapter 3, "The Business Value of Better Requirements," addresses the question of what return on investment managers can expect if their organizations get serious about improving the way they approach requirements. Chapters 4 and 5, "How Long Do Requirements Take?" and "Estimating Based on Requirements," deal with the ever-thorny issue of estimation. Chapter 4 discusses some of the factors that indicate whether a project team should expect to spend more or less time than average developing its requirements. Chapter 5 presents three approaches to estimating the size of the project's requirements collection. Requirement size estimates then feed into estimates of the effort needed to implement the corresponding functionality. But remember, these aren't predictions—they're estimates.

Chapter 3
The Business Value of Better Requirements

Managers often ask me what return on investment (ROI) they can expect from the money they spend on training, process improvement, and tools for requirements engineering. I can't give them a nice, tidy answer. As with so many questions in software, the correct answer is, "It depends." You can send everyone in your organization through the best training, develop the greatest processes, and buy top-tier tools. The biggest determinant for ROI, though, is whether the project teams actually *do* anything differently regarding requirements engineering now that they have these new capabilities. Your organization won't derive much benefit from this considerable investment if team members continue to work in the ways they have in the past. In this chapter, I discuss some of the factors that contribute to determining what ROI an organization can expect from better requirements.

Tell Me Where It Hurts

Not every manager is convinced that his team needs to do a better job on requirements development and management. Numerous industry studies, however, indicate that requirements issues are a pervasive cause of project distress. The often-quoted CHAOS Reports from The Standish Group indicate that three of the biggest factors that lead to failed or challenged[1] projects are:

- Lack of user input.

- Incomplete requirements and specifications.

- Changing requirements and specifications.

---

1. "Challenged" projects deliver a product that is late, is over budget, has reduced features, or has some combination of these shortcomings.

A recent example of requirements failure was the Federal Bureau of Investigation's new case-management software system, VCF. This project was abandoned after $170 million had been spent on it because the delivered software was full of defects and off-target functionality. An investigation by the U.S. General Accounting Office pointed to a principal cause of this expensive failure (Goldstein 2005). According to one author of the GAO's report:

> I suspect what happened with the VCF is that in the rush to put in place a system, you think you got your requirements nailed, but you really don't. It was a classic case of not getting the requirements sufficiently defined in terms of completeness and correctness from the beginning. And so it required a continuous redefinition of requirements that had a cascading effect on what had already been designed and produced.

Various studies have examined the effects of errors in requirements on software projects. One study at a large defense contractor found that 54 percent of all software defects were discovered *after* unit testing was complete; 45 percent of these defects were attributable to requirements or design errors (Boehm et al. 1975). Forty-one percent of all errors discovered on a U.S. Air Force systems development project originated in the requirements (Sheldon et al. 1992). Similarly, a recent survey of 12 companies determined that 48 percent of all their software project problems were related to requirements (Hall, Beecham, and Rainer 2002). The typical outcome of errors in the requirements is an expectation gap: a difference between what developers build and what customers really need.

The age of the Internet has, if anything, made the requirements problem worse. A 2001 survey "confirms that e-projects are time-compressed, intensive, and mission-critical efforts with poorly defined requirements" (Rodrigues 2001). The top three risks that threatened the success of the e-projects surveyed were:

1. Unstable, constantly changing requirements (reported by 66 percent of the survey respondents).

2. Poor requirements specification (reported by 55 percent).

3. Client behavior, such as approval delays, requirements changes, and poor communication (reported by 42 percent).

Clearly, any domain that is the root cause of approximately half the problems on software projects deserves careful attention.

The main reason errors in requirements are so damaging is that they force the development team to perform extensive rework to correct them. Multiple studies have shown that the cost of correcting a software defect increases dramatically the later it is discovered, as shown in Table 3-1 (Boehm 1981; Grady 1999). That is, it can cost 68 to 110 times more to correct a requirement defect found in operation than it would if that same defect had been discovered during requirements development. An error, omission, or misunderstanding in the requirements forces developers to redo all the work they've already done based on the incorrect requirement. Therefore, any technique that can reduce requirement errors and prevent some of this wasted effort is a high-leverage investment indeed. One analysis of the potential return on investment from better requirements suggests that requirement errors can consume between 70 and 85 percent of all project rework costs (Leffingwell 1997).

Table 3-1   Relative Cost to Correct a Requirement Defect

Stage Error Was Discovered	Relative Cost to Correct
Requirements development	1X
Design	2–3X
Construction	5–10X
System or acceptance test	8–20X
Operation	68–110X

What Can Better Requirements Do for You?

In addition to avoiding some of the negative consequences described in the previous section, better software requirements provide numerous benefits. These include helping your organization select the right projects to fund, facilitating estimation, enabling rational prioritization, helping developers create higher-quality designs, and making testing more effective.

Selecting projects to fund   Good preliminary requirements enable senior managers to make effective business decisions as organizations decide which among a set of potential projects to fund. Better requirements allow more accurate projection of business returns. Once a project is funded, better requirements allow project managers to more sensibly partition tasks among their teams and even among individual team members.

Facilitating estimation   Well-understood and well-documented requirements can help your team estimate the effort and resources needed to execute a project. (See Chapter 5, "Estimating Based on Requirements.") Reliable estimation requires some historical correlation between requirements size and effort. A simple count of requirements is a useful starting point, but it's more valuable to consider the relative size and complexity of the requirements when relating them to the total development effort.

Enabling prioritization   A comprehensive set of requirements allows the team to prioritize its remaining work. Most projects need to make compromises to ensure that they implement the most critical and most timely functionality. A well-understood and prioritized requirements baseline also helps the team incorporate those changes that will deliver the maximum customer value. One study revealed that just 54 percent of the originally defined features were delivered on an average project (The Standish Group 2003). If you can't implement all the requested functionality, make sure the team implements the right parts.

Developing designs   Requirements serve as the foundation for product design. Therefore, well-understood and well-communicated requirements help developers devise the most appropriate solution to the problem. High-quality requirements also ensure that the development team works on the right problem. Many developers have experienced the frustration of implementing functionality that a customer swore he needed, only to find that no one ever executed that functionality. One survey indicated that 45 percent of the delivered software product features were *never* used (The Standish Group 2003). Wasting less time implementing the wrong functionality accelerates the project and maximizes its business return.

Testing effectively   Requirements provide the reference for system testing. Well-defined and testable requirements enable the testers to develop accurate test procedures to verify the functionality. Prioritizing requirements tells testers which requirements to concentrate on first. Assessing requirement difficulty and risk helps testers know which functionality should receive the closest scrutiny.

A comprehensive, traced set of requirements helps the stakeholders know when the project is finished. A body of work is complete when all the requirements allocated to it are either verified as having been correctly implemented in the product or deleted from the baseline. Defined business requirements also allow the stakeholders to determine whether the project has met its goals.

Believe it or not, investing more effort in developing the requirements can actually accelerate software development. This seems counterintuitive, but it's true. Following are some examples:

- In a study of 15 banking and telecommunications projects, the most successful project teams spent 28 percent of their resources on requirements engineering, whereas the average project team in the study devoted just 15.7 percent of its effort to requirements (Hofmann and Lehner 2001).

- Increasing the fraction of the total budget devoted to requirements on a group of NASA projects led to substantially lower overruns of both cost and schedules (Hooks and Farry 2001), as depicted in Table 3-2.

Table 3-2   Cost and Schedule Overruns on Some NASA Projects

Percent of Budget Spent on Requirements	Number of Projects	Average Project Cost Overrun
Less than 5	5	125%
5 to 10	7	83%
More than 10	6	30%

- At a large insurance company I worked with, increasing the front-end effort (project definition plus requirements) on small maintenance projects from 19 percent of total effort to 33.6 percent reduced the overall project effort and cost by an average of 4 percent.

- In a European survey, the fastest project teams spent twice as much of their schedule (17 percent versus 9 percent) and effort (14 percent versus 7 percent) on requirements activities as the slower teams (Blackburn, Scudder, and Van Wassenhove 1996).

■ After another of my clients, a large manufacturing corporation, trained its development teams on requirements engineering and implemented improved requirements practices, its project schedule performance improved significantly. Over a span of one year, the fraction of projects that were behind schedule dropped from 21 percent to just 12 percent. Furthermore, the cumulative days that projects were behind plan dropped from 1,738 days to only 518 days one year later.

Good requirements practices can accelerate development in several ways. Defining business requirements—the expected business outcomes the product will provide—aligns the stakeholders with shared vision, goals, and expectations. Effective user involvement in establishing the requirements reduces the chance that users will reject the new system upon delivery. Accurate requirements ensure that the functionality built will enable the users to perform their essential business tasks. The requirements also define achievable quality expectations. This lets the team implement both the capabilities and the product characteristics—the nonfunctional requirements—that will make users happy. Additionally, emphasizing requirements development is cheaper than relying on beta testing to find requirements problems. Fixing problems so late in the game is far costlier than correcting them earlier.

The Investment

If you want to determine the ROI from any new activity, you need to track both what you invested in the activity and the benefits—such as reduced costs, accelerated schedules, or increased sales—you enjoyed as a result. Unfortunately, few software organizations collect this sort of data. It's not hard to track the money and time your organization spends developing improved requirements. Measuring the payback is trickier. Following are some of the actions you might take to improve your requirements process and hence the product requirements themselves. Record what you spend on these activities to determine your investment.

■ **Assessing current practices**   All process improvement should begin with some kind of appraisal. You need to learn how your teams are dealing with their requirements issues today and how those current approaches do and do not yield the desired results. You might begin with the "Current Requirements Practice Self-Assessment" available at *http://www.processimpact.com/goodies.shtml*, also described in Appendix A of *Software Requirements, Second Edition*.

■ **Developing new processes and templates**   Once you've identified specific requirements engineering practices that are ripe for improvement, your teams need to devise processes that will work better for them. This might involve writing new processes, modifying current processes, and selecting or adjusting the templates for your key requirements deliverables. You can start with the sample templates for a vision and scope document, use case document, and software requirements specification available from *http://www.processimpact.com/goodies.shtml*. Adapt these to meet your project needs as appropriate.

- **Training the team**   It's not reasonable to expect your team members to work in new ways if they haven't been taught how to perform the new practices. All analysts and others who must deal with project requirements should receive some basic training in requirements engineering concepts and practices. The team members also need training in the effective use of your own processes and templates.

- **Acquiring books and other resources**   Requirements engineering is a complex domain with many concepts and practices. Your analysts will benefit from having reference books and articles on hand so that they can refresh their knowledge and get ideas for handling new challenges they encounter. Books are a high-yield investment, assuming that team members actually read them and apply what they learn.

- **Employing external consultants**   Some software organizations pursue improved requirements approaches on their own. Others prefer to acquire assistance from experienced consultants who have worked with a variety of companies. Consultants are not cheap, but they can help your team members solve problems much faster than they might on their own.

- **Buying requirements management tools**   Written requirements documents have numerous limitations. As your requirements engineering activities become more sophisticated, you might elect to store requirements in a database rather than in traditional word-processing documents. More than 25 commercial requirements management tools are available. Descriptions and comparative information are available at *http://www.paperreview.com/tools/rms/read.php* and *http://www.volere.co.uk/tools.htm*. These tools make it far easier to store attributes that provide readers with a rich understanding of each requirement, to track requirements status, to deal with changes, and to record requirements traceability information. If you acquire such a tool, be sure to train your team in its effective use. See Chapter 23, "Exploiting Requirements Management Tools," for tips on getting the most from your tool investment.

The greatest investment you make in developing superior requirements is the time your team members spend eliciting, analyzing, documenting, validating, and managing the requirements for the products they're creating. As you saw in the previous section, investing this time is likely to shorten your project development cycle, amply rewarding the additional investment in quality requirements.

The Return

I can't predict what ROI you're going to get from your investment in better requirements. There are too many variables, most of which depend on the performance of your teams. However, I can help you think through what the payback might be for your organization.

The return you can expect to receive depends on the price your projects are currently paying for shortcomings in your requirements. If your teams are forced to perform extensive rework to deal with overlooked or inaccurate requirements, you'll obtain a better return than if requirements issues are just a minor nuisance. Before you dive into requirements process improvement, consider the following questions:

- What fraction of your development effort is expended on rework? (Few software organizations can answer this question. Those that have measured it find that rework can consume 30 to 50 percent of all the effort expended on a software project. Some rework is unavoidable and adds value [Fairley and Willshire 2005] but much rework constitutes wasted effort.)

- How much does a typical customer-reported defect cost your organization? A defect found through system testing? (Every organization should know this. To my knowledge, only one of my clients has measured this cost, though. That client spent an average of $4,200 to deal with each customer-reported defect. Contrast this with their average cost of just $200 to discover a defect by inspection and correct it.)

- What fraction of user-reported defects and what fraction of defects discovered through system testing originate in requirements errors? (Identifying the root causes of defects is an excellent technique for determining where your leverage lies for quality improvement.)

- How much of your organization's maintenance costs—such as defect correction and unplanned enhancements—can be attributed to missed requirements or other types of requirement defects?

- How much do you think you could you shorten your delivery schedules if your project teams could reduce requirement defects by, say, 50 percent?

The goal of software process improvement is to enhance the bottom line of your business by lowering the costs of building and maintaining software. Adopting practices that result in fewer requirement defects will reduce the amount of development rework your teams must perform. Performing less unnecessary rework has a direct payback through reduced product development costs and quicker time to market. Techniques that get your analysts and customers working closer together lead to products that better meet customer needs. Superior requirements development also lowers your maintenance and support costs. If requirements fall short, many products have to be modified immediately after release when the customers realize some critical functionality is missing or wrong.

Besides these obvious practical benefits, improving your requirements approaches leads to other valuable, but less tangible, outcomes. Experiencing fewer miscommunications on a software project reduces the overall level of chaos. Less chaos lowers unpaid overtime, increases team morale, boosts employee retention, and improves the team's chances of delivering on time. And all the benefits I've described here have the potential of leading to higher customer satisfaction. What is that worth to you? It might be hard to measure, but it's real.

An Economic Argument

A sign in a high-school chemistry lab reads, "If you don't have time to do it right, when will you have time to do it over?" We rarely take the time to understand a product's requirements clearly enough to reduce the risk of racing into construction. However, companies nearly always find the time, money, and resources needed to fix a flawed product. The case for emphasizing solid requirements practices is an economic argument—a business argument—not a philosophical or technical position. Think about how your company's bottom line is affected by requirements-related problems. Then use that understanding to justify investing in better requirements practices that can pay off for the long term.

Chapter 4

How Long Do Requirements Take?

Analysts and managers sometimes ask me how long it will take to perform requirements development on their next project. There is no fixed answer to the question. Multiple variables contribute to this issue. Various industry averages have been published to suggest what percentage of a typical project's effort should be devoted to requirements development. Data from different benchmarks don't agree very well, though, and whether these "typical" projects are similar to your own is questionable.

Industry Benchmarks

Here's an illustration. Table 4-1 presents some industry benchmark data for the average percent of total effort and the average schedule time that projects in several different categories devote to requirements elicitation and prototyping (Jones 2000). These benchmarks are for very large projects of 10,000 function points in size (approximately one million lines of code). How similar are your projects to these benchmarks?

Table 4-1   Benchmarks for Requirements Work on Large Projects

Project Type	Percent of Total Effort on Requirements Development	Months Spent on Requirements Development
Management information systems	3.7	4.44
Systems software	9.0	13.2
Commercial products	7.0	22.7
Military software	10.0	17.5
Outsourced projects	9.0	21.9

There's another problem with using industry benchmarks such as those shown in Table 4-1. The data doesn't indicate how successful those projects were or define what "success" means for each project. Nor does this data indicate whether the more successful project teams devoted more of their effort to requirements activities than the less successful teams—they're just averages of actual performance.

Whereas typical project teams devote perhaps 10 percent or less of their effort on requirements, investing more has a big payoff, provided the team doesn't get trapped in analysis paralysis. Contrary to what many people believe, spending more time on requirements can actually accelerate software development. Chapter 3, "The Business Value of Better Requirements," presented some data supporting this conclusion.

 While working on small projects when I was employed at Kodak, my team would typically devote 15 to 18 percent of our total effort on requirements activities (Wiegers 1996). We found this investment reduced the amount of post-delivery rework we had to do. It's difficult to link causes and effects with certainty, but I believe the greatest contributing factor to our low maintenance level was the extensive user participation we cultivated.

I can't tell you how long you should expect to spend on requirements development for *your* next project. However, Figure 4-1 identifies some of the conditions that can accelerate requirements development and several other factors that lengthen the time needed for effective requirements development.

Less Time	**More Time**
• Highly skilled and experienced analysts • Extensive customer involvement with appropriate user representatives • Reuse from previous projects • Customer representatives who respond quickly to questions • Clear and stable vision and scope • Developers experienced in application domain • Replacing a legacy application • Effective incremental peer reviews to remove ambiguity and find omissions	• Unfamiliar project or application domain • Geographically distributed stakeholders • Language barriers between project participants • Weak decision-making process • Large project • Many or diverse user classes • Concurrent software development and business process reengineering • External dependencies and uncertainties • Complex interactions between hardware and software components • No requirements development process in place

Figure 4-1   Factors that influence the time needed for requirements development.

Your Own Experience

Your best bet is to collect some data on how much of your own project effort is spent on requirements development and to judge how well that has worked for you in the past. (See Chapter 22, "Measuring Requirements.") Use this historical data when estimating the requirements effort needed for future projects. Adjust your initial estimate by using the considerations in Figure 4-1 to compensate for differences between your next project and the benchmark projects. Consider any additional factors that would influence your own project. You might weight each of the factors shown in Figure 4-1 on a scale of 0 (no effect) to 5 (major impact). This analysis can help you spot risk factors that could prolong your requirements development work.

Another factor to consider is the development life cycle that the project is following. Not all the requirements effort should be allocated to the beginning of the project, as is the case in the sequential or waterfall life cycle. Don't think in terms of a discrete "requirements phase," but rather about a set of requirements-related activities that span the project's life cycle. In particular, requirements management will be performed on an ongoing basis once a set of requirements is baselined and change requests begin to appear.

Incremental Approaches

Projects that follow an iterative life cycle will include requirements development at every iteration. Projects using the iterative Rational Unified Process (RUP) will devote considerable effort to the requirements workflow during the early Inception phase and particularly during the Elaboration phase (Ambler and Constantine 2000a). As Ambler and Constantine (2000b) point out regarding RUP's Elaboration phase, "The basic idea is that your goal is to understand the core 80% of the system that you are building—you might be missing a few details, but you understand what it is that you are trying to build." In this model, requirements activity continues at a reduced intensity level throughout the iterations in the later Construction and Transition phases.

Projects that follow one of the contemporary agile development methodologies (such as Extreme Programming, Scrum, and Adaptive Software Development) take an incremental approach, rapidly building small portions of the product. This puts potentially useful functionality in the users' hands quickly so that users can refine their needs and developers can keep up with changing business demands. Agile projects will have frequent but small requirements development efforts.

 Many years ago, one of my software development group's successful projects took just such an incremental approach. This project released useful functionality to the internal corporate user community every three weeks. The first part of each three-week cycle was spent on project planning and developing the requirements for that increment. The team did just enough requirements development for that increment, quickly implemented it, and provided new functionality to the users one piece at a time. The users provided feedback on those increments, which helped steer the rest of the project toward delivering maximum value.

Not all projects are amenable to such fine-grained incremental delivery. When reengineering an existing application, for instance, the new system needs a critical mass of functionality before users can switch to it. Regardless of how large an increment your team tackles on each project cycle, they need to understand the requirements for that increment to avoid extensive rework of designs, code, and tests.

Planning Elicitation

As with so many aspects of software projects, there's more to requirements development than initially meets the eye. As you're identifying the tasks your analysts might need to perform, consider whether activities such as the following will be necessary:

- Negotiating commitments with product champions.

- Holding elicitation workshops and conducting interviews.

- Reviewing existing documents and products.

- Preparing, distributing, and analyzing surveys.

- Creating and evaluating prototypes, analysis models, and other requirements views.

- Performing feasibility, risk, safety, failure, and hazard analyses.

- Entering requirements information into a database.

- Reviewing requirements specifications.

- Developing test cases from requirements and walking through the test cases.

- Revising requirements specifications following review or test analysis.

Your team might not perform all these activities on each project, and they might have to do other tasks as part of requirements elicitation, analysis, specification, and validation. Anything you learn about the tasks the analysts actually perform and how long those tasks take will improve your ability to estimate the requirements development effort needed for future projects.

Chapter 5
Estimating Based on Requirements

Nearly all software project teams must estimate the effort, time, and cost required to execute their projects. Estimation is a difficult challenge for which no magic solution exists. As with all technical practices, you'll get better at estimation with experience, but only if you study how closely your estimates match the actual results. A full tutorial on software estimation is beyond the scope of this chapter. For a comprehensive discussion of estimation, see Steve McConnell's *Software Estimation: Demystifying the Black Art* (2006). In this chapter, I describe some estimating approaches and three specific techniques for generating estimates based on requirements.

Some Estimation Fundamentals

An estimate is a prediction of some aspect of the future, given certain knowledge and certain assumptions at a specific time. Because this information is incomplete and imperfect, and because unexpected events will occur, estimates have uncertainty. This is why they're called *estimates* instead of *predictions*. Managers and other stakeholders often want highly accurate and precise estimates early in the project, but that is simply not possible because of the unavoidable uncertainty.

The earlier in the project an estimate is produced, the less accurate it will be. Estimates generated from preliminary high-level requirements will have more uncertainty than estimates produced from a detailed requirements specification. As the project continues, you can produce increasingly accurate estimates for the amount of work remaining. However, the only time you will know exactly when you'll be able to deliver is the moment before you do.

Figure 5-1 illustrates the *cone of uncertainty* that reflects the increasing accuracy of estimates made at the end of later project phases (McConnell 1998). A value of 100 percent on the y-axis indicates the actual outcome. The error bar in the figure illustrates that an estimate produced after preliminary design is complete should be viewed as having an uncertainty range of about +40 percent and −30 percent. This conical effect is similar to the storm track that weathermen forecast for hurricanes. As the weathermen look farther into the future, the uncertainty of exactly where the hurricane will be at a specific time increases.

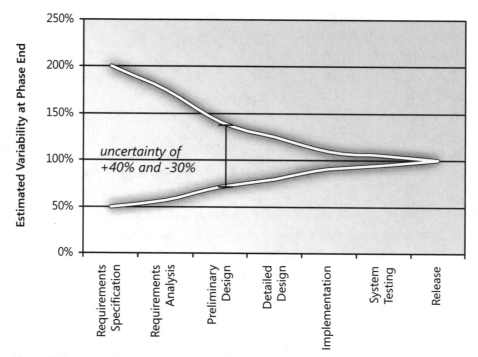

Figure 5-1   Cone of uncertainty for project effort estimates.

Because of the uncertainty, it's a good practice to report estimates as a range, not as a single point. A single-point estimate conveys an overly precise expectation to the person who receives that estimate. Suppose your manager asks you for an estimate based on preliminary requirements and you reply, "Ten months." How likely do you think it is that the project will really be done 10 months from now? One hundred percent? Ten percent? That single-value answer gives your manager no clue about your confidence in the estimate or the estimate's uncertainty.

But suppose you prepare a careful estimate, based on benchmark data from previous projects and perhaps using some estimation tool. This analysis leads you to conclude that there's a

50 percent probability that you could complete the project in about 10 months, an 80 percent chance it would be done in 12 months, and only a 10 percent likelihood that it would be done in eight months. Rather than picking one of these durations as "the estimate," be honest about the uncertainty.

An estimate is really a probability distribution. You could provide a table or a chart such as that shown in Figure 5-2, which illustrates the probability of being finished by each of those times. This reflects the uncertainty both in the estimation process and in your knowledge of what the product will ultimately become during the course of the project.

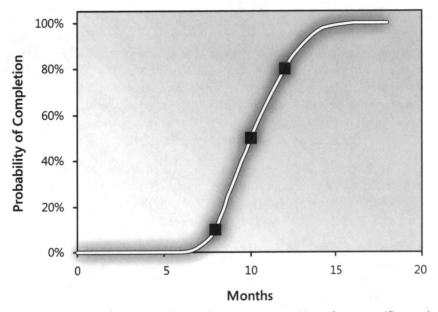

Figure 5-2   Cumulative probability of completing a project after a specific number of months.

Admittedly, most managers are less happy with estimates that have fuzziness around them than with highly precise single-point estimates. Nonetheless, the reality is that estimates *are* uncertain. Let's deal with reality, however distasteful it is. If you need to estimate exactly when your company will be able to sell the product, you'll need to include contingency buffers to account for the estimation uncertainty. False precision in an estimate implies unjustified accuracy.

Estimation Approaches

Several estimation techniques can be applied to software projects. Following is a brief summary of some of those methods.

Bottom-up   Bottom-up estimation is based on a breakdown of the project into individual elements, each of which is estimated separately. Project elements could consist of individual requirements, tasks, or deliverables from a work breakdown structure, or counts of items such as classes, program modules, or test cases. The estimates for the individual elements are then compiled to get an estimate for the entire project.

Top-down   Top-down estimation begins with a description of the product or project as a whole. The estimator judges what it would take to execute the entire project, based on previous experience with similar projects. This overall estimate is then allocated among the subcomponents to estimate the size, effort, time, or cost needed to implement each individual element.

Cost models   Many commercial estimating tools are available. These incorporate algorithms derived from many completed projects of various types. The algorithms correlate some project outcome, such as effort or schedule, with factors such as product size, product characteristics, team productivity, team size, and so on. The estimation tools allow you to provide descriptive information about your product or project. They then calculate a number of possible outcomes based on the algorithms using a statistical simulation. These outcomes represent various combinations of effort and schedule that are equally probable. The cost models reflect the reality that nonlinear tradeoffs exist between the various parameters. For example, doubling the size of the team does not cut the schedule in half.

Expert opinion   Experts who have worked on projects similar to the one being estimated judge what it would take to implement the new project. The estimate generated depends very much on the expert. It's also important to understand the assumptions the expert is making, such as which individuals will be working on the project.

Analogy   Estimating by analogy is a matter of comparing the new project to a set of previously executed projects. Does the new project seem to be about the same size as the last one, or is it bigger or smaller by a certain percentage? Are there specific characteristics that make the new project significantly different from the previous ones, such as a change in technologies used or delivery platform? The actual effort, schedule, and cost of the reference projects are used to generate estimates for the new project based on their similarities to and differences from the new project. Of course, this requires that actual performance data from those previous projects be available. Top-down and expert-opinion estimates could be derived from analogy-based estimation.

Wideband Delphi   The Wideband Delphi estimation technique involves a group of estimators who make their initial estimates independently and then converge iteratively toward an acceptable estimate range as they combine their knowledge (Wiegers 2000). It's essentially a multi-expert opinion method that mitigates the risk of asking only one expert for an estimate. In a Wideband Delphi session, several estimators develop their own task lists, an estimate for each task, a list of assumptions, and an overall, bottom-up estimate for the project. The individual estimates are shared anonymously within the estimation group so that the estimators aren't influenced by another participant they might view as having more insight into the project. The participants modify their task lists, estimates, and assumptions through several rounds of refinement until the results represent a sensible range of possible outcomes.

Each of these estimation methods is useful in certain circumstances. Consider developing multiple estimates using different techniques. Significant disconnects between multiple estimation methods suggest that something has been overlooked in one of the estimates or that different estimators made different assumptions.

Goals Aren't Estimates

Tutorials on estimation typically are presented as though the necessary functionality is already defined and the purpose of estimation is to determine the corresponding effort, cost, time, and staff needed. Sometimes estimation works the other way, though. If the schedule is constrained such that the product absolutely must be delivered by a particular date, the relevant estimation parameter is how much functionality of given quality will fit into that time box. It's important to recognize that a management-imposed or marketing-imposed delivery schedule is *not* an estimate; it is a goal. A team of a certain size and skill level can produce only so much high-quality functionality in a fixed time.

 I once met a project manager who was delivering a new release of his product every three months. His team came up with a list of committed features they knew they could implement in the next quarter, as well as a prioritized list of "stretch" features. They would complete the committed features and then implement as many of the stretch features as they could before the scheduled delivery date arrived. This is an example of coping effectively with uncertain estimates through intelligent scope management in a time-boxed development cycle.

Estimating from Requirements

One bottom-up estimation strategy is to begin with knowledge about the product's requirements and then estimate the resources and time needed to implement those requirements. The rest of this chapter describes several ways to do this. You might prefer to generate macro-level top-down estimates for the entire project. But if you do want to produce more comprehensive and accurate estimates, these methods can help.

A fundamental estimation equation is:

```
Effort = Size ÷ Productivity
```

The size of the product, and hence the size of the project, depends on the size of the requirements. To estimate the effort needed to complete a body of work, then, you need some measure of requirements size, along with knowledge about the development team's productivity. Productivity indicates what quantity of functionality the team can realistically implement in a development iteration of a given duration. The previous equation provides a first-cut estimate of effort. The schedule estimation process then looks like this:

1. Estimate the size of the requirements by using one of the techniques suggested in the next section.

2. Calculate the team's productivity by correlating the size of several previously implemented, similar products with the total effort needed to implement them.

3. Estimate the new development effort based on this previous productivity data or, if no hard data is available, based on estimated productivity.

4. Adjust this preliminary effort estimate to reflect significant differences between the new project and the benchmark projects used to calculate productivity. Consider factors such as product complexity and risk, team experience in the application domain, development methodologies and tools used, and schedule pressure. (Remember that tired people work more slowly and make more mistakes.)

5. Assuming that this effort estimate encompasses all the work necessary to complete the project, translate that effort into calendar time. This is not a simple matter of dividing the total effort in staff-hours by a nominal 40 hours per week. The actual hours devoted to project effort is typically in the range of 60 to 70 percent of the total at-work hours. When one of my software groups at Kodak measured our effective project hours for several years, our weekly average never exceeded 31 hours per week (Wiegers 1996). Calendar time estimates also depend on delays that could take place while waiting for someone to complete a review, make a decision, answer a question, or supply a deliverable.

6. Incorporate contingency buffers into the effort, cost, and schedule estimates to account for the possibility of estimates being low, project scope increasing, risks materializing, and other unexpected events taking place (Wiegers 2002c).

Measuring Software Size

The central premise of this estimation approach is that we have some way to judge the size of the software. Unfortunately, there is no perfect measure of software size. Following are several possible software size measurements.

Lines of code   You might be able to estimate this by analogy from previous projects, but lines of code aren't related directly to requirements size.

Function points   Function points are an indirect, abstract measure of software size that can be estimated from requirements and user interface design information (IFPUG 2002). Calculating function points involves counting the number and complexity of five elements found in information systems: external inputs, external outputs, internal logical files, external interface files, and external inquiries. The initial function point count is adjusted by rating 14 characteristics of the project and the development team. Function points don't work well for systems that have a fairly simple set of inputs and outputs but a lot of processing complexity under the hood. Learning to count function points accurately is a specialized skill, but many organizations have found this to be a valuable size measurement, particularly for information systems.

3D function points   3D function points extend function points to measure attributes from the three dimensions of data, function, and control (Whitmire 1995). This enhancement makes the function point method more applicable to real-time systems.

Story points   Some approaches for agile software development employ user stories (described in the next section) as the unit of requirements, rather than functional requirements or use cases. Thus, user story points serve as a measure of requirements size.

Use case points   The analyst can assess the number and complexity of use cases[1] to get a measure of requirements size, and hence product size (Karner 1993; Ribu 2001). Use case points are adapted from the function point counting method.

Counts of testable requirements   Peter Wilson proposed that analysts write functional requirements at a consistent level of granularity that he describes as being individually testable requirements (1995).

The rest of this chapter describes using counts of story points, use case points, and testable requirements to estimate the size of your requirements. As Figure 5-3 illustrates, these three methods represent requirements at increasing levels of detail available at increasingly later stages of the project.

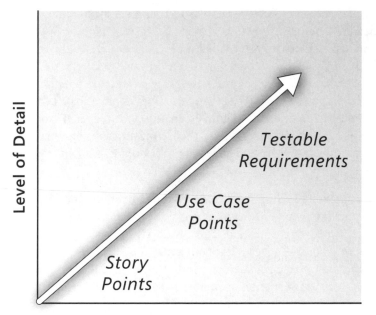

Figure 5-3   More detailed requirements representations permit more precise estimates.

1. See Chapter 9—"Use Cases and Scenarios and Stories, Oh My!"—for an overview of use case concepts and terminology.

Story Points

Some agile software development methodologies, such as Extreme Programming, represent software requirements in the form of *user stories*. A user story "describes functionality that will be valuable to either a user or purchaser of a system or software" (Cohn 2004). The story consists of a brief written description, conversations that provide additional details, and tests that are used to document those details. These high-level requirement representations are available early in the project.

Story points indicate the size and complexity of a given user story relative to other stories that are part of the project (Cohn 2004). No standard definition of a story point exists. Each development team is free to define a story point as they wish. Cohn favors treating a story point as "an ideal day of work," although this is actually a measure of effort, not size. A story point might be defined more precisely as the amount of functionality a developer could implement in an ideal day of work without considering interruptions and other ways that time is spent besides on project work. One developer's "ideal day of work" might be quite different from another's. Multiple studies have shown that software developers demonstrate at least a tenfold range of individual productivity (DeMarco and Lister 1999).

Determining the number of story points in each story is subjective. There's nothing you can count directly to get the number of story points. Also, different analysts will write stories at different levels of detail. Therefore, estimating story points is essentially an application of the expert opinion estimation technique. Each estimator's judgment is based on his own interpretation of how large the story will be (recognizing that it is initially stated at a high level and will be elaborated and perhaps subdivided) and how long it would take to implement a typical story of that size. Cohn recommends having several developers participate in a story point estimation activity, similar to a Wideband Delphi estimation session. Such group estimation reveals differences of opinion about story size and the factors and assumptions that went into each estimate. This helps the team agree on how many story points they are confronting for a given product release.

An agile project's development iterations are time-boxed to a fixed duration, typically two to four weeks. Project estimation, then, is a matter of considering how many story points a team can implement and verify in a single iteration. This productivity measure of story points per iteration is termed *project velocity*. The team does not commit to implement more story points in a given iteration than their previous experience indicates is feasible, based on their project velocity measures. Because the user stories are defined at a fairly high level, more uncertainty is associated with their implementation estimates than for more fully specified requirements.

Strangely, velocity is based on the originally estimated story points, regardless of whether a story winds up taking substantially longer than the team initially thought it would. A better approach would be to use the actual story point results to determine a more realistic velocity to use for estimating subsequent iterations.

Use Case Points

A use case contains considerably more information than a user story but less detail than a functional requirements specification. Use case points were developed by Gustav Karner (1993) as a way to measure software size by quantifying the number, size, and complexity of the product's use cases.

Figure 5-4 shows the process flow for calculating use case points. Use case points consider both the complexity of the use cases themselves and the actors that interact with the use cases.[2] The initial point count is modified based on several technical and environmental factors to produce a count of adjusted use case points. Following is a detailed description of how to count use case points. This is more complicated to explain than it is to perform, especially with the help of a simple spreadsheet.

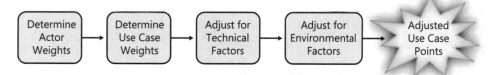

Figure 5-4   Process for calculating use case points.

Actor Weights

First, identify the actors that will interact with the system through use cases. Different types of actors contribute different weighting factors to the count of use case points, as shown in Table 5-1.

Table 5-1   Use Case Point Contributions from Actors

Actor Type	Description	Weighting Factor
Simple	Another system that interacts through a defined application programming interface (API)	1
Average	Another system that interacts through a protocol such as TCP/IP, or a human actor that interacts through a simple command-line user interface	2
Complex	A human actor that interacts through a graphical user interface	3

---

2. An *actor* is an entity outside the system's scope boundary that interacts with the system by initiating or participating in the execution of certain use cases. To a first approximation, an actor is a user, but there are subtle distinctions between them. See Chapter 10, "Actors and Users."

Classify all the actors by whether they are simple, average, or complex. Multiply the number of actors of each type by the corresponding weighting factor and total the results. This yields the *unadjusted actor weights* (UAW) that will contribute to the use case point total. Consider a hypothetical system that has four use cases that are executed by three human actors (weight of 3×3). The system also interacts with three external systems through APIs (3×1) and one external system through a communication protocol (1×2). The unadjusted actor weights (UAW) are calculated as follows:

```
UAW = (3*1) + (1*2) + (3*3) = 14
```

Use Case Weights

Next, rate the complexity of each use case as shown in Table 5-2. Complexity is based on how many "transactions" each use case encompasses. Different writers have different definitions of what constitutes a transaction within a use case. I recommend that you count each normal, alternative, and exceptional flow in a use case description as one transaction. You would never implement just a part of a flow, so it makes sense to treat each flow as a unique transaction.

Table 5-2   Use Case Point Contributions from Use Cases

Use Case Type	Number of Transactions	Weighting Factor
Simple	1–3	5
Average	4–7	10
Complex	more than 7	15

Various flows within a given use case might have different priorities. You might implement only the normal flow and its associated exceptions in the first release, two alternative flows and their exceptions in the second release, and so on. Treating flows as the atomic element for sizing use cases allows you to count the use case points planned for a particular release. The first time you implement part of a use case will involve the most effort because you need to write code to test preconditions, enforce business rules, satisfy postconditions, and so forth.

Suppose the use case portfolio for your system consisted of the four use cases described in Table 5-3. Each use case has a single normal flow, zero or more alternative flows that also lead to successful outcomes, and some exceptions that could potentially cause the use case execution to fail. If we define each successful and exception flow as one transaction, our four sample use cases have the total number of transactions shown. Applying the weighting factors from Table 5-2 gives the number of *unadjusted use case weights* (UUCW) shown in Table 5-3 for these use cases. The total number of *unadjusted use case points* (UUCP) is the sum of the unadjusted actor weights and the unadjusted use case weights:

```
UUCP = UAW + UUCW = 14 + 45 = 59
```

Table 5-3   **Unadjusted Use Case Points Example**

Use Case Number	Normal Flows	Alternative Flows	Exception Flows	Total Transactions	Use Case Weights
1	1	0	2	3	5
2	1	1	5	7	10
3	1	5	12	18	15
4	1	3	7	11	15
Total Unadjusted Use Case Weights					**45**

Technical and Environmental Factors

Finally, we need to modify the unadjusted use case points according to several factors that affect how much work it will take to implement a body of requirements (Karner 1993). Table 5-4 lists 13 nonfunctional requirements and other technical factors that could affect development productivity and their relative weights. Rate your project by how strongly each of these items affects it, using a scale of 0 (irrelevant) to 5 (strong influence). A column of sample ratings is included for illustration, continuing our example in this section. The sum of these weighted ratings gives the *TFactor*, or technical complexity factor.

Similarly Table 5-5 identifies an additional eight environmental factors that can also modify productivity. These issues have to do with the programming environment, development team, requirements stability, and other considerations. Their weighted sum is called the *EFactor*, or environmental factor.

Table 5-4   **Technical Factors Affecting Use Case Points**

Factor ID	Description	Weight	Sample Rating	Sample Value
T1	Distributed system	2	3	6
T2	Response time or throughput performance requirements	1	2	2
T3	End-user efficiency	1	5	5
T4	Complex internal processing	1	2	2
T5	Reusability	1	1	1
T6	Installability	0.5	2	1
T7	Usability	0.5	5	2.5
T8	Portability	2	1	2
T9	Modifiability	1	4	4
T10	Concurrency	1	0	0
T11	Includes special security requirements	1	3	3
T12	Provides direct access by third parties	1	4	4
T13	Special user training facilities are required	1	0	0
Total TFactor				**32.5**

Table 5-5   Environmental Factors Affecting Use Case Points

Factor ID	Description	Weight	Sample Rating	Sample Value
E1	Familiarity with life-cycle model used	1.5	4	6
E2	Application domain experience	0.5	2	1
E3	Experience with development methodologies used	1	4	4
E4	Analyst capability	0.5	2	1
E5	Team motivation	1	4	4
E6	Stability of requirements	2	3	6
E7	Use of part-time team members	−1	0	0
E8	Use of difficult programming language	−1	1	−1
Total EFactor				21

The sum of the weighted technical factors leads to a Technical Complexity Factor (TCF) according to the following equation:

`TCF = 0.6 + 0.01*TFactor = 0.6 + (0.01*32.5) = 0.925`

The sum of the weighted environmental factors produces an Environmental Factor (EF) in a similar fashion:

`EF = 1.4 - 0.03 * EFactor = 1.4 - (0.03*21) = 0.77`

The constants in these equations—0.6 for the TCF calculation and 1.4 for the EF calculation—were presented in Karner's original paper on use case points (1993). They represent his assessment of the impact these factors have on the effort required to implement a use case. The final calculation of *adjusted use case points* (UCP) for the system uses the following formula:

`UCP = UUCP * TCF * EF = 59 * 0.925 * 0.77 = 42.0`

Determining Your Productivity

Now you know how to count up the use case points to be implemented in your next project. But how fast can your team implement these use cases? You need to establish a correlation between size (measured in use case points) and effort so that you can determine your team's productivity.

Some literature on use case points suggests that you should plan on 15 to 30 labor hours to implement a single use case point. You could use this range as a *very* rough estimate, but your mileage may vary significantly. As always, the best bet is to calculate your own productivity from previous measures of project effort and size. If you have historical effort data available, you can go back and count the use case points from the completed project.

Suppose that correlating effort with use case points indicated that your teams require an average of 28 labor hours (*not* calendar hours!) to implement one use case point. Your effort estimate for implementing our sample system with four use cases then would be:

```
Effort = (42.0 UCP) * (28 hours/UCP) = 1176 labor hours
```

Problems with Use Case Points

Use case points seem to be relevant to many types of projects. However, this method does have some limitations you should keep in mind:

- There is considerable variation in how practitioners write use cases. Use cases can be described at a high level of abstraction or in great detail. Some use cases show just the actor's view of what's going on with the system; others include internal processing details that aren't visible to the actor. To get consistent use case point counts, your analysts will need to document use cases in a consistent style.

- Use cases aren't an effective requirements development technique for all types of systems. (See Chapter 11, "When Use Cases Aren't Enough.") For instance, suppose the bulk of the complexity lies not in the actor-system dialogs (for which use cases are well-suited) but in the computations that the software performs. Use cases then would give a misleadingly low measure of the system complexity, for which the "complex internal processing" technical factor (T4 in Table 5-4) only partially compensates.

- Use cases might not capture all the necessary system functionality. (See Chapter 11.) Size measures based only on use cases would then underestimate the true size of the product.

As you gain experience applying use case points to your projects, you'll develop sensible heuristics for how to adjust the method to suit your situation. For example, suppose you have a simple use case that has only three transactions but involves complex business rules. You might call that an average use case or a complex use case to more accurately estimate how large the project really is.

You might also be able to take some estimation shortcuts. Perhaps you learn that, on average, your use cases work out to 11 use case points each. If the same team is working on a series of similar projects or a sequence of incremental releases, you might assume that the technical complexity and environmental factors remain constant. This will let you generate an initial effort estimate based simply on the number of use cases you identify and these historical averages.

Testable Requirements

The idea behind testable requirements is that the analyst can decompose functional requirements through levels of progressive refinement until each one is precisely defined, unambiguous, and verifiable. That is, a tester could think of a small number of logically related test cases that would verify whether a particular requirement was correctly implemented. If all the functional requirements in an SRS are decomposed to a similar level of granularity, the number of individually testable requirements is a measure of the size of the system (Wilson 1995). (See *http://www.testablerequirements.com/testablerequirements/index.htm* for more information about testable requirements.)

In my reviews of many requirements specifications, I've seen the full gamut of granularity. A requirement for one project said:

A valid color code shall be R for red.

This is a tiny requirement.[3] At the other extreme, I once saw a single functional requirement in an SRS that contained about 700 requirements that stated:

The Editor shall respond to editing directives entered by voice.

Can you think of two or three logically related test cases to verify this requirement? More like 200 or 300, I think. This single "functional requirement" is alluding to a speech recognition component, which could be enormously complex. Such a requirement should be decomposed into several additional levels of detail to understand the full scope of what it means.

The concept of deriving testable requirements helps answer the question of how detailed the requirements need to be. (See Chapter 13, "How Much Detail Do You Need?") Testable requirements also provide a way to track your project status. You can assign a status attribute to each testable requirement, which could have values such as Proposed, Approved, Implemented, Verified, Deleted, and Rejected (Wiegers 2003a). This attribute lets you monitor the number of functional requirements that have each status at a given time. And what could be a more basic metric for your requirements engineering activities than the number of discrete requirements? (See Chapter 22, "Measuring Requirements," for other requirements-related metrics.)

The next step for estimation would be to establish a correlation between total project effort and the number of testable requirements. One of my software teams performed such an analysis for several small systems we had implemented. We found that on average, implementing a single functional requirement consumed 5.6 hours of labor effort (Wiegers 1996). This effort included all project activity between baselining the requirements specification and releasing the system. This data provided a measure of our productivity that we used to estimate future similar projects. We still needed to adjust those estimates for significant differences from the benchmark projects that could affect our productivity on the next project, though.

Rather than assuming that your organization's productivity is similar to that of my old group, collect some data from your own projects and establish a suitable correlation for your own

---

3. Actually, it's not a functional requirement at all but rather a data definition that states an allowed value for a data item called *color code*. But it appeared in an actual SRS as a functional requirement.

team's work. If you do not already have such requirements and project effort data available, there's no time like the present to begin collecting it. Someone asked me once where to get historical data for estimation. If you write down what you did today, tomorrow that will be historical data. It's as simple as that.

The Reality of Estimation

Just as you'll never develop a perfect set of requirements, you'll never develop perfect estimates for how long it will take to implement your requirements. There will always be uncertainties, and the requirements will always change and grow during the course of the project. The estimation process leads to tensions between various stakeholders. Managers and customers often demand faster delivery than is reasonable. Developers can be overly optimistic about their own performance. Estimators are sometimes accused of padding their estimates to make it more likely that they will finish on time.

Sensible project management requires good faith, objectivity, and analysis to judge the size of the work to be performed and how fast the team realistically can be expected to work. Whenever you're participating in a negotiation, having data available strengthens your negotiating position. It's harder to argue with historical data on team productivity than with some stakeholder's perception of how quickly a project ought to be executed. Watts Humphrey (1998) provides several practical suggestions for how to participate in such a data-driven negotiation.

Your best estimation strategy is to adopt a consistent way of measuring the requirements size and to collect data from enough projects so that you're confident that your team is making achievable commitments. If you do not collect data to use when preparing estimates, you will never be estimating; you will always be guessing.

Part III
On Customer Interactions

It's no secret that the extensive and continuous engagement of appropriate customer representatives is a critical success factor in software development. Part III sheds some light on specific aspects of customer participation.

Agile development methodologies frequently use the phrase *on-site customer*. I applaud the concept, but I disagree with the implication that a single individual can be found to serve as the voice of a diverse customer base in most situations. Instead, Chapter 6, "The Myth of the On-Site Customer," proposes using a small group of product champions to work with requirements analysts to develop and validate requirements. Chapter 7, "An Inquiry, Not an Inquisition," suggests many questions the analyst might ask when working with customer representatives to develop both business and user requirements. The chapter describes the purpose of each question so that you can think about how to adapt them to suit your personal interviewing style.

Reviewing the requirements specifications and associated deliverables is a vital element of customer engagement. Unfortunately, busy customers often don't participate constructively—or perhaps at all—in requirements reviews. Chapter 8, "Two Eyes Aren't Enough," suggests some strategies that might increase the chance that the right people will take the time to find requirements errors at an early stage through peer review.

Chapter 6
The Myth of the On-Site Customer

The agile software development methodology known as Extreme Programming has as a central tenet the premise that every project needs a full-time, on-site customer who sits with the developers (Jeffries, Anderson, and Hendrickson 2001). The rationale is sound. Only knowledgeable and empowered customer representatives can answer questions and flesh out high-level requirements in appropriate detail. Failing to get timely answers or clarification holds up development and forces the developers to make their best guess. Customers also can provide quick feedback on proposed user interface displays, clarify points of confusion, and resolve conflicting requirements or priorities.

I fully endorse the premise of intimate, ongoing engagement of appropriate customer representatives on software projects. Many studies have shown that insufficient customer involvement is a common cause of project failure. My concern about the phrase *on-site customer* is simply that it is singular. It suggests that a single individual is available who has sufficient knowledge, expertise, and authority to make requirements decisions on behalf of the entire user community. This individual must also have considerable time available to devote to the project. Even if you could find one such highly qualified representative, other demands will compete for his time unless he and his management make participation in the project a priority.

User Classes and Product Champions

In reality, most products have multiple—often many—distinct *user classes*, groups of users who have largely different needs. Certain groups—the favored user classes—will be more important than others to the business success of the project (Gause and Lawrence 1999). It's unlikely that any one person will be able to represent the needs of all the user classes and to appropriately balance their interests when making decisions and reconciling conflicts.

A more realistic approach is to enlist a small number of *product champions* to serve as key user representatives (Wiegers 2003a). In 1985, my small software group at Kodak adopted the product champion approach with great success (Wiegers 1996). In this model, the primary communications bridge across which user requirements flow involves one or more analysts working with one or more product champions, as Figure 6-1 illustrates.

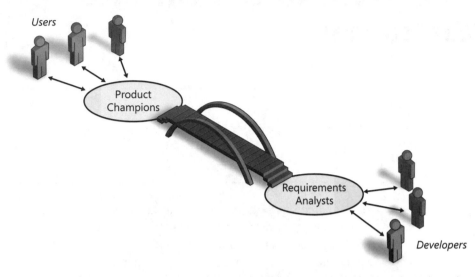

Figure 6-1 The requirements communication bridge connects analysts and product champions.

As a first approximation, look for one product champion per major user class. Some individuals might be members of multiple user classes and could present the needs of all those groups. In other situations, large user classes might be divided logically into sub-user classes. I once encountered this situation on a project that involved building an information system to track chemical usage. Our largest user class was a community of several hundred chemists. We found an experienced chemist, Don, who could supply most of the requirements for the common needs of these chemists. Don served as the primary interface between that user class and the requirements analyst (me) working with the chemists on the project. The product champion communicated with other members of his peer group to identify requirements, propose suggestions, and resolve conflicting input. If any other self-appointed champions approached me with input (mostly solution ideas, not requirements), I'd ask them to work with Don.

During this project, though, we learned that certain small groups of chemists throughout the company had some specialized needs. We lined up several other chemists to work with Don to ensure thorough coverage of the community's requirements. Don was first among equals, though. If this group of representative chemists couldn't all agree on some issue, Don made the call and we all respected his conclusion. Someone has to make these kinds of decisions. Ideally, a knowledgeable and respected user representative will do it. Otherwise, the analyst or developers must make their best guess, which isn't a reasonable burden to place on them.

On this same project, we had three other important but much smaller user classes. We found a product champion to represent each of these other groups. The four product champions together served as our "voice of the customer." Ideally, your champions will be co-located with the analysts and developers for the duration of the project so that they can quickly answer questions and supply the myriad details that written requirements specifications lack. This is the intent of the on-site customer principle. In practice, none of our product champions ever spent more than about 25 percent of their time working on our projects. Nor were they co-located with the analysts and developers, although they were accessible enough to provide quick feedback when necessary.

I've spoken to many analysts and developers who have tried the product champion model. I've also met users who have served in this role. They invariably report that the approach was highly successful, provided four conditions are met:

- The right individuals assume the product champion role.

- Each champion understands and signs up for his responsibilities. (See Chapter 6 of *Software Requirements, Second Edition* for some typical responsibilities.)

- Each champion has the time available to do the job.

- Each champion has the authority to make binding decisions at the user requirements level.

Simply having an on-site customer doesn't guarantee that he'll provide the expected contribution. My colleague Julia learned this the hard way. Julia's original product champion was co-located with the developers yet failed to interact with them in the expected way. This negated the value of having a customer on site. Julia acquired a new champion who interacted much more effectively with the developers and strongly influenced the project's direction. The key message from this experience is that it's essential for your customer representatives to commit to making the type of project contributions you need from them.

Surrogate Users

The ideal product champion is an actual member of the user class he represents. This isn't always possible, particularly when building commercial products for a faceless market. You might need to use surrogates in place of real user representatives. Perhaps a product manager can fill this role or a local subject matter expert can speak for the users. Even in a commercial environment, someone must provide the necessary requirements input. This could mean that a product manager is acting as the product champion. In such a situation, it's still useful to identify your user classes and explicitly determine who the literal voice of the customer is for each class. That said, try to avoid the following user surrogates:

- **Former members of the user class**   Their perceptions of user needs and how current users would employ the system could be obsolete. However, they might be able to do a good job if they're still in touch with current users or if the application domain hasn't changed substantially since they were active users. One of my clients was building a software product to manage the point-of-sale and back-office operations for photo studios. The company hired three former photo studio managers as regular employees to serve as product champions. As soon as these people joined the company that was developing the product, they were no longer managing photo studios. Perhaps their knowledge of photo studio needs was still current enough to be valuable, though.

When your product champions are former users, you have to ask yourself whether a significant disconnect will grow over time between their perceptions and the actual user needs. Some industries change quickly and others change more slowly. Just be aware of the possibility of a growing gulf of current knowledge between users and their representatives.

■ **Managers of the real users** Managers sometimes are leery about delegating decision-making authority to ordinary users. They're also reluctant to have valuable employees spend a lot of time working with the software development team on the faith that this will pay off eventually. Sometimes managers say, "I did that job myself for 10 years. I can tell you everything you need to know." But there are two problems with this rationale. First, those managers are not current members of the user class. Second, busy managers rarely have the time to devote to a serious requirements development effort. They'll likely resent the many interruptions a fully engaged customer representative can expect to receive. It's better to have managers provide input to the *business* requirements and ask them to identify some current members of the user class to contribute to the *user* requirements.

■ **Software developers who think they can speak for the users** This situation will rarely work. More commonly, even developers with considerable domain experience will find that actual future users of the new product will bring a different perspective. Of course, if the product is intended to be used by software developers, your own developers might be perfectly reasonable user representatives. It's a good idea for members of any product development organization to employ its own products in their work or their daily lives whenever possible. This is called eating your own dog food. Don't just simulate a user— be one!

■ **Personas** Some organizations have had success with creating *personas* as stand-ins for actual users (Cooper 1999). A persona serves as an archetype of a particular user class. A persona provides a description of the behavior you can expect from representative members of a particular user class, including a description of their goals and character-istics. Using a carefully crafted persona to explore requirements and design decisions might be better than appointing an actual person who has too many biases to serve as a representative user.

Now Hear This

Your stakeholders might hesitate to invest the considerable time it takes to have knowledge-able users work with requirements analysts and developers. Here's how I see it: You're going to get the customer input eventually. It's a lot less painful to get it early on, as well as on an ongoing basis during development. The alternative is to wait until the system is released, hear about all the things the analysts and developers did wrong, and then spend a lot of time, money, and goodwill fixing those problems.

I encounter many teams that would love to have more customer involvement but are deliberately blocked from talking to actual users. This is a special concern when the customer is not himself an end user yet prevents the developers from interacting directly with users. In other cases, no one is willing to spend the time to work with the development team on requirements, prototype evaluations, or other opportunities for engagement. If you can't get your customers or their surrogates to invest time in making sure the product meets their needs, I seriously question their commitment to project success.

In an ideal world, a single, full-time, expert user would indeed be sitting within view—"on sight"—of developers, ready at a moment's notice to speak definitively for the entire user community. In reality, this is unlikely in most situations. More realistically, the project manager and requirements analyst should assemble a small group of product champions who can properly interpret and balance the needs of the user classes they represent. Then build a close, collaborative relationship with those product champions so that you can get the VOC—the voice of the customer—as close as possible to the EOD—the ear of the developer.

Chapter 7
An Inquiry, Not an Inquisition

Many years ago, my manager at the time, Jerry, sat in on a discussion I had with a customer named Steve to explore his requirements for a new process-control application. After the meeting, Jerry pointed out that I had been rather aggressive in my questioning of Steve. He was right. I hadn't realized how hard I'd been pressing Steve to make up his mind on certain points and tell me exactly what he wanted. Fortunately, when I contacted Steve to apologize it was clear that he wasn't offended. Nonetheless, our discussion probably felt like an inquisition to Steve, rather than an inquiry into what he was asking us to build.

Another extreme approach to requirements elicitation is for the analyst to simply record whatever the customer says and pass that information on to the developers. As with most things in life, the appropriate behavior lies in between the possible extremes.

Requirements elicitation is an exploration and discovery process, and the requirements analyst is the guide. Analysts need to recognize that customers won't be able to deliver all their requirements in a single workshop or discussion. Elicitation requires multiple cycles of refinement, clarification, and adjustment as the participants move from high-level concepts to specific details, perhaps through a series of releases or iterations. This chapter describes some questions an analyst might consider asking during an elicitation discussion—and some to avoid. *Exploring Requirements: Quality Before Design* by Donald Gause and Gerald Weinberg (1989) is a classic resource of good questions for discussing requirements for any type of project.

But First, Some Questions to Avoid

The worst question you can ask during a requirements discussion is, "What do you want?" The second-worst question is, "What are your requirements?" No one knows quite how to answer these questions. Customers and other elicitation participants might not share the analyst's understanding of what a "requirement" is. When customers attempt to answer these questions in good faith, they typically generate a large number of random—yet important—thoughts.

This happens in some of my training seminars, in which small groups of students conduct a practice requirements elicitation workshop on a sample project called the Cafeteria Ordering System. The groups are supposed to be learning how to apply use cases to explore user requirements. One member of each group plays the role of a user who would employ this system to order meals. Some groups begin by asking this student, "What do you want?" because this is how they're accustomed to launching requirements discussions. They typically get responses such as the following:

- I must be able to pay by credit card and payroll deduction.

- I want to be able to order group meals for lunch meetings.

- The system has to be available from home as well as from work.

- I need to submit delivery instructions.

- The system should tell me if an item I selected is no longer available at the instant I submit the order.

- I shouldn't have to pay any delivery charges.

- Can contractors order meals or just employees?

- I want to be able to order meals at least a week in advance.

- It would be nice if I could reorder the same meal I ordered sometime in the past.

- Could I get nutrition information for a whole meal?

These are unquestionably important thoughts that the customer has. However, they're spewed out in a random sequence with no organizing structure. This makes it hard for both the analyst and the customer to know what to do with the information, where to store it, and what to discuss next. The student groups who take this approach invariably flounder in the sea of random input, whereas those groups that grasp the use case approach make much more progress. An important analyst skill is to structure the dialogue and ask questions that will guide elicitation participants through progressive layers of refinement in an organized fashion.

The analyst should remember his role as a neutral facilitator. We all filter what we hear through our own biases, preferences, experiences, and hot-button issues. Avoid asking leading questions that steer customers to agree with your own intentions. Also avoid overruling a customer's idea just because it doesn't agree with your own point of view. I once observed a 60-participant "voice-of-the-customer" workshop that a client conducted to explore requirements for a major new product. The workshop facilitator was the senior manager responsible for the product. He had strong opinions about the project's direction and didn't hesitate to steer the discussion toward his predetermined outcomes. This is discouraging for participants, who will feel that they're wasting their time if the facilitator already knows what the answers will be.

Questions for Eliciting Business Requirements

We explore business requirements to gain a shared understanding of the business opportunity being created or exploited, business objectives, success criteria, product vision, and project scope boundaries. Business requirements answer the question, "Why are we undertaking this project?" Sources of business requirements include senior managers, marketing managers, funding sponsors, product visionaries, and others who know the rationale and business drivers for the new product. Following are some questions to consider asking if you're an analyst working with these holders of the business requirements.[1]

What business problem are you trying to solve?   This question helps align subsequent requirements development and software development activities with the right objective.

What's the motivation for solving this problem?   Team members work together more effectively if they understand the rationale behind their work.

What would a highly successful solution do for you?   Management should be able to state the benefits they and their customers will receive from the product.

How can we judge the success of the solution?   People often don't think about how they will determine whether some enterprise has been successful. Contemplating this evaluation early on helps crystallize the stakeholders' thinking about objectives and steers the project toward a clearly successful outcome.

What's a successful solution worth?   Whenever possible, quantify the business outcomes (Wiegers 2002b). All projects involve some cost-benefit analysis. Understanding the potential return in measurable units helps participants make cost-effective decisions.

Who are the individuals or groups that could influence this project or be influenced by it?   This question seeks to identify potential stakeholders in the project. These stakeholders might need to be consulted to understand their interests in the project, their expectations, and the nature of their involvement.

Are there any related projects or systems that could influence this one or that this project could affect?   Look for dependencies between projects and systems that need to be analyzed and accommodated. Sometimes small changes can have huge ripple effects across multiple interconnected systems.

Which business activities and events should be included in the solution? Which should not?   These questions help define the scope boundary. Modifying the established project scope is a business decision that has implications for cost, schedule, resources, quality, and tradeoff decisions. See Chapter 17, "Defining Project Scope," for suggestions about how to document the scope boundary.

---

1. Some of the questions in this chapter were stimulated by work performed by consultant Esther Derby, *http://www.estherderby.com*.

Can you think of any unexpected or adverse consequences that the new system could cause? Consider whether certain individuals, organizations, customers, or business processes could experience a negative impact from the system or product being developed. For example, a new information system that automates a process that has been performed manually in the past could threaten the job stability of the people who perform that process. Employees might need retraining, or their job descriptions could change, both of which could lead to resistance to the project and unwillingness to cooperate.

User Requirements and Use Cases

The business requirements will help the analyst identify potential user classes for the product. The objective of exploring user requirements is to understand what the members of these user classes expect to be able to do with the product and how the product will enable them to achieve specific goals. The user goals must align with the higher-level business goals captured in the business requirements.

Some user goals might pertain to tasks the users must perform; use cases are an effective way to record these tasks. Other user goals, though, might indicate the importance of specific nonfunctional requirements. Examples include the ability to complete a task within a certain length of time and the ability to access a system remotely from a cell phone or other wireless device. Therefore, user requirements also encompass the users' expectations about performance, availability, usability, reliability, and other quality attributes. It's also important to surface pertinent business rules, design and implementation constraints, and assumptions the various stakeholders might be making. The objective is for the analyst to understand what customers are envisioning so that the analyst can record both functional and nonfunctional requirements that will guide the development team's work. Furthermore, documented requirements and user acceptance criteria will help testers determine whether the delivered product satisfies its requirements.

When eliciting user requirements, the requirements analyst typically works with a number of key users who represent specific user classes. (See Chapter 6, "The Myth of the On-Site Customer.") The analyst needs to ask questions that will help those users describe the goals they want to accomplish with the help of the system. For most types of software projects, this is far more valuable than the traditional focus of requirements discussions on system features and functions. The emphasis on user tasks or goals is the essence of the use case approach to requirements elicitation.

Instead of asking, "What do you want?" or even "What do you want the system to do?" an approach based on usage and user goals asks, "What do you need to do with the system?" Your users might not be accustomed to a dialogue of this nature. It can be difficult to shift their thinking from the traditional focus on the system itself. Some education of your user representatives is in order. It's not realistic to think you can simply ask the users what their use cases are and get a meaningful response. Even if you explain what use cases are, don't expect users to give you a tidy, precise, and complete list of their use cases. The analyst must work with the input that users provide to determine the real goals they have in mind.

I often use the example of an airline flight reservation kiosk when describing use cases in my training seminars.[2] Instead of just asking the class what their use cases would be for a system such as this, I ask them, "What are some things you would imagine doing with an airline flight reservation kiosk?" A variant question is, "What are some reasons you would want to use an airline flight reservation kiosk?" During a class discussion, some of the responses are indeed use cases, although they still need to pass through a filter that asks "Is this in scope?" before we determine that they belong in the system we're exploring. These use cases include:

- Find Available Flights for an Itinerary.
- Make a Flight Reservation.
- Select Seats.
- Print an Itinerary.
- Change a Reservation.
- Cancel a Reservation.
- Check on Flight Status. (This one might not be in scope because it requires real-time access to current flight information from the airlines. The business requirements should indicate whether this sort of capability will help us achieve our business objectives.)

Notice that all these use cases begin with a verb. This is a standard convention for naming use cases. The analysts should listen for responses from customers that do not begin with a verb and discuss the intent behind each such response. Once when I held this discussion in a class and asked, "What are some things you would imagine doing with an airline flight reservation kiosk?" one student simply said, "Weather." This one-word response prompted me to explore exactly what aspect of weather the student had in mind; we needed to find an appropriate verb. Did she want to *create* the weather, *change* the weather, or what? After a brief discussion, I determined that she wanted to *check* the weather forecast at the originating, destination, and connection cities for a specific flight itinerary. We can't use a software system to change the weather, but we might be able to check the weather if this capability is deemed to be in scope for the project. Hunting for the verb the customer has in mind is a way to discover the task or goal behind the initially presented input.

Just because a user provides a response that begins with a verb doesn't mean that it's actually a use case. When discussing the airline flight reservation kiosk, a student will often suggest as a possible use case, Enter My Frequent-Flier Number. A use case should describe a

---

2. For some reason, airline flight reservation systems and automated teller machines are commonly used to illustrate use cases. They must have seemed reasonable to me also, because I began using the same examples long before I read my first book on use cases. These common products represent systems with which many people have experience, so practitioners and customers alike can relate to the kinds of things users would do with them.

standalone task: A user has a specific goal in mind, walks up to the system, interacts with it in some way, and—if all goes well—achieves the goal and walks away happy. However, no one would ever walk up to this kiosk, enter his frequent-flier number, and feel satisfied. Certainly, the idea of entering his frequent-flier number had some meaning to the student who proposed it, but it does not represent a use case in its own right. I needed a follow-up discussion to determine what the user was really trying to accomplish by entering a frequent-flier number. There could be several reasons for someone to enter his frequent-flier number:

- See how many miles he has accrued.

- Purchase a ticket using frequent-flier miles.

- Purchase a seat upgrade using frequent-flier miles.

- See if he has qualified for premium-level frequent-flier status.

- See if he has received mileage credit from a previous flight, car rental, or hotel stay.

- Recall his stored profile so that he doesn't have to reenter a lot of information when making a reservation.

- Indicate which frequent-flier account should receive the miles from an upcoming flight.

The first five of these items are use cases, something a user might do as a standalone task. The last two, though, don't represent discrete tasks. They are part of some other use case, such as Make a Flight Reservation. The main point here is that the analyst must expect to work with users to determine whether a piece of presented input is a user task, a bit of system functionality, a quality attribute, a constraint, a business rule, extraneous information, or something else.

Questions for Eliciting User Requirements

Following are several sets of questions the analyst might consider asking customer representatives during a discussion about user requirements. Don't use these questions as a script to be followed by rote in an elicitation workshop. Instead, look for ways to build these sorts of questions into the natural flow of a requirements exploration.

What are some reasons why you or your colleagues would use the new product?
These "reasons to use" could become candidates for use cases. They might identify business tasks or objectives that members of a particular user class might need to achieve from time to time.

What goals might you have in mind that this product could help you accomplish?
Use cases normally are directed toward helping the user achieve a specific goal. The name of the use case indicates the goal the user has in mind: Print a Boarding Pass, Withdraw Cash, Calibrate Pressure Meter, Submit an Employment Application, and so on. Users can't always articulate their goals directly, though. Observation and other techniques, such as contextual inquiry (Beyer and Holtzblatt 1998), might be necessary to discover what users really expect.

What problems do you expect this product to solve for you?   Understanding the problems and limitations the users perceive in their current environment helps analysts determine the appropriate capabilities for the new system. This question also helps determine whether the end users' objectives for the system align well with senior management's objectives, as captured in the business requirements. Users might expect the system to do something for them that is out of scope according to senior management's judgment. Such a disconnect points to the need for iteration between the business requirements and user requirements levels. The key stakeholders must hold aligned expectations for the new or modified product.

What external events are associated with the product?   Analysts sometimes use the term *business event* to describe the triggering condition that launches execution of a use case. Perhaps a help desk receives a phone call from a user who needs assistance. This external event triggers the help desk staffer to create a problem report ticket. Create Problem Report Ticket is a good name for a use case. In other types of products, such as real-time control systems, use cases are not a valuable technique for understanding user requirements. An alternative approach is to identify the external events the system must detect. Then describe the appropriate system response, which depends on the state the system is in at the time each event is detected. See Chapter 11, "When Use Cases Aren't Enough," for more about events.

Most requirements discussions focus on functionality. However, a product's nonfunctional characteristics also have a great impact on how users feel about the product. Questions such as the ones that follow help the analyst understand the user's expectations about aspects of the product's quality.

What words would you use to describe the product?   Consider asking users to close their eyes and describe their vision of the future system. Listen to the words they use to describe the product. Nouns suggest objects the system must be able to manipulate (such as order, reservation, chemical, account balance, sensor). Verbs can indicate actions the user expects to be able to take or expects the system to take (such as place, create, revise, submit, receive, detect, measure, display). Adverbs convey the user's thoughts about the product's characteristics (for example, quickly, reliably, efficiently, flexibly, easily). Use this input to better understand what the user considers to be important about the product.

Are specific portions of the product more critical than others for performance, reliability, security, safety, availability, or other characteristics?   As much as we might like to, software developers can never create a product that combines the maximum levels of all quality characteristics. Tradeoffs are necessary between properties such as usability and efficiency, integrity and usability, and integrity and interoperability. Therefore, it's important to understand which specific portions or aspects of the product have critical quality demands so that the developers can optimize their designs to achieve those objectives. Sure, everyone would like 100 percent availability in all locations, but that's not realistic. It's quite likely that certain system functions or use case flows have more stringent availability requirements than others. Certain flows will have rigid response-time requirements, but others will not be time-critical. Perform this same analysis for the other quality attributes.

Are there any constraints or rules to which the product must conform?   Most products are subject to corporate policies and technical standards, industry standards, government laws and regulations, and other external constraints. These are collectively referred to as *business rules.* (See Chapter 21, "Business Requirements and Business Rules.") It's essential to know about the pertinent business rules so that analysts can specify functional requirements to enforce or comply with those rules. Don't expect users to present all these rules spontaneously. The analyst needs to identify where such rules are likely to be pertinent and to explicitly ask users about them. Business rules sometimes fit into a company's oral tradition or folklore; the rules are very real but they might not be documented. Look for subject matter experts within the organization who have current knowledge about the business rules.

How is the product you envision similar to the way you do business now? How should it be different?   When automating current business processes or replacing an existing information system with a new one, it's easy to inadvertently re-implement all the shortcomings of the current approaches. This is known as "repaving the cow paths." It's difficult for people to break from the mindset of their current ways of working and to envision something that's really different and better. The analyst should stimulate the thinking of the user representatives to help them fully exploit this opportunity to devise better ways of working. Rethink business rules and business processes to see what has changed—or what could change.

What aspects of the current product or business process do you want to retain? To replace?   This question is similar to the previous one. Customer acceptance of a new product depends partly on how comfortable and familiar it feels to them. Similarity to previous products and processes reduces the learning curve, making it easier for users to master a new system and workflow. Knowing which aspects of the current business process or software system irritate the users reveals opportunities for improvements that will delight customers.

The following questions also help the analyst gain a richer understanding of how potential users view the product. Asking these questions of people who represent different stakeholder groups can reveal disconnects or conflicts that must be reconciled when defining and prioritizing the product's functionality.

Which aspects of the product are most critical to creating business value?   A user's view of business value might be different from a manager's view or an acquiring customer's view. A user might value a more efficient way to perform a specific task that will save considerable time over many executions. A manager, on the other hand, could be more impressed if the product has lower acquisition and support costs than the one it is replacing.

What aspect of the product most excites you?   The answers to this sort of question help analysts determine what product characteristics or capabilities could be powerful enablers of customer acceptance.

What aspect of the product will be most valuable to you? Least valuable?   No project can deliver everything to everybody on day one. Someone needs to prioritize, to determine the sequence in which to implement various capabilities. Ask this question of different user representatives, and look for patterns that indicate certain product capabilities are more important and more urgent than others. Those capabilities should have top priority.

What is most important to you about the product?   The deliberately general way this question is phrased could generate responses dealing either with the product itself or with other aspects of the project. One user might say, "It's most important that this system be available before the beginning of the next fiscal year." Another user might respond, "It's most important that this system will let me import all my data from these older systems we've been using." A manager might say, "It's most important that the people in my department can get up to speed on this new system with little or no training." These responses have implications for how the project is planned, the product functionality to include, and usability, respectively.

How would you judge whether the product is a success?   A business manager might judge the success of the product quite differently from how members of different user classes determine success. Surface these different perspectives early so that they can be reconciled and so that you keep all stakeholders working toward a common objective.

Can you describe the environment in which the product will be used?   The operating environment has a big impact on both requirements and design decisions. The operating environment will provide information about possible external interfaces that must be constructed. The user interface is also highly sensitive to the operating environment. Touch screen displays are superior to keyboards in some settings, for example, and speech recognition is becoming increasingly effective. But speech recognition wouldn't work well in an environment with a lot of background noise.

Open-Ended Questions

The analyst is not simply a scribe who records whatever a customer tells him. The analyst needs to stimulate the thinking of the people he's interviewing to get below the surface. The analyst should ask questions such as "What else could happen that we haven't already discussed?" and "Would anyone ever want to <do something>?" and "Could <some scenario> ever occur?" These are ways to discover possible alternative pathways that represent lower-probability scenarios or options the system should provide to the user.

In their classic book *Exploring Requirements*, Gause and Weinberg describe "context-free questions" (1989). In their words, context-free questions "are high-level questions that can be posed early in a project to obtain information about *global* properties of the design problem and potential solutions. Context-free questions are completely appropriate for any product to be designed." These questions can be used to explore both processes and products. They're a valuable complement to specific questions about the capabilities and characteristics of the product being explored.

In my experience, requirements elicitation discussions typically emphasize the expected normal behavior of the system. However, anyone who has ever programmed knows that a lot of code is written to deal with exception conditions. An important aspect of requirements elicitation is to identify things that could go wrong, determine how the system should detect an error, and describe how the system should respond to the error. As an analyst, you need to probe around the exceptions during your requirements discussions. Ask questions such as, "What should happen if <some error condition arises>?" This is a way to detect missing requirements that haven't come up in the discussion yet. It's also a way to surface previously unstated assumptions. Testers are particularly adept at spotting exception conditions.

Beware of asking questions that solicit a yes/no or multiple-choice type of response. Such questions can unnecessarily constrain the answer so that the requirements discussion misses an opportunity to discover (or invent) something that goes beyond the analyst's preconceptions. Of course, this doesn't mean you can't ever ask a question with a closed list of possible responses. Just make sure you aren't prematurely constraining the exploration.

The last question I typically ask in a requirements elicitation discussion is, "Is there anything else I should be asking you?" This is an example of a *metaquestion,* a question about a question (Gause and Weinberg 1989). I freely admit that I don't know all the right questions to ask. Sometimes the person of whom I've asked this question realizes that we haven't yet discussed some important topic. I simply didn't know enough to bring it up.

I use this same question when I'm a customer in daily life. I recently had new kitchen counters installed in my house. I'd never done this before and didn't know that much about the process. Near the end of my discussion with a contractor, I asked, "Is there anything else I should be asking you about this job?" He thought for a moment and then brought up an issue we had not yet discussed. This is also a collaborative question to ask. It acknowledges that you rely on the expertise of other people to work toward a mutually satisfactory project outcome.

Why Ask Why?

"Why?" is an excellent question to put in the analyst's bag of tricks. During a reengineering project, an analyst named Dawn asked one of the developers why a utility company fee calculation was being performed a certain way in the existing system. "There's a governmental statute that dictates how we have to calculate these fees," was the reply. Upon investigation, Dawn discovered that in fact the current system had not implemented the computation correctly according to that statute. The utility fees had been calculated incorrectly for an embarrassingly long time. This discrepancy never would have come to light had Dawn simply accepted the stated need for the current computational formula. Asking why revealed a major error that the replacement system corrected.

The shrewd requirements analyst asks why a lot. It's important that "why" explorations be expressed in a way that doesn't sound confrontational, accusatory, or challenging (Derby 2004). I often ask questions that begin this way: "Can you please help me understand..." This phrase is longer than *why* and means essentially the same thing, but it has a more collaborative feel to it.

When a user representative presents a requirement containing an embedded solution idea, asking why can let you know whether the solution idea is a true design constraint or just a suggestion. Asking why several times in succession is a way to drill down from a proposed customer "want" to the real underlying need. This helps the software team address the real issue, not just a superficially presented issue. Gently probing with *why* can reveal other sorts of useful information:

- The answer to *why* might point out a business rule that affects the project. Then you can check to see whether the business rule is still pertinent and whether the information you have available for it is complete and accurate. You can discover whether and where the business rule is documented, who's responsible for maintaining the information, and whether there are related rules you need to know about.

- Asking why sometimes surfaces assumptions held by the person you're questioning. An assumption is a statement that you regard as being true in the absence of definitive knowledge that it *is* true. It's important to try to identify assumptions that various stakeholders might be making. Those assumptions could be incorrect or obsolete. They could be at odds with assumptions other people are making. Such conflicts make it harder for the stakeholders to have shared project expectations.

- Asking why can reveal implicit requirements that no one thought to mention yet.

- The answer to "Why is this requirement included?" supplies the rationale behind the requirement. It's always a good idea to know where each requirement came from and why it needs to be included in the project. This can help the analyst learn about requests that lie outside the project scope. This question sometimes also exposes that the "requirement" is really a design idea for an unstated higher-level requirement.

- Suppose you encounter a requirement that a user representative presented as being of high priority. It doesn't look that important or urgent to you. If you ask why it's high priority, perhaps you'll learn that it's logically connected to other requirements that also are high priority. Without this knowledge, someone might unwittingly defer the requirement that doesn't seem so important, thereby crippling the dependent requirements that are scheduled for early implementation.

- Sometimes the analyst thinks he understands a requirement, only to discover upon further investigation that he really doesn't. Asking why a requirement is necessary a few times could provide additional details that solidify the analyst's understanding of that requirement.

- Asking why or similar questions can help the analyst distinguish essential knowledge from extraneous information.

 Asking why might save you a lot of work. One project was replacing an existing customer relationship management (CRM) system with a package solution. Senior management directed the team to use out-of-the-box features from the package as much as possible and to limit the extent of configuration or changes to the package. One user representative asked that a specific function be added, a counter that indicated how many times a customer had used a certain product feature. It would have cost a significant amount to modify the core package to accommodate this requirement. When the analyst asked why that function was needed, she was told that the function was present in the current CRM application. The analyst probed further: "What exactly does this counter show?" "Why do you check it?" "What action do you take depending on what it tells you?" This discussion eventually revealed that several stake-holders all thought that someone else was using the data. In reality, no one used it at all! By asking "why" a few times, the analyst and user representative agreed that the function wasn't needed, thereby saving a significant amount of money.

As an analyst, you need to be a bit of a skeptic. Don't believe everything you hear, and don't accept it all at face value. Ask "why" enough times to give you confidence that you've got the real requirements in hand.

Chapter 8

Two Eyes Aren't Enough

In this chapter:

In my view, the most powerful quality practice available to the software industry today is inspection of requirements documentation. A *peer review* is an activity in which someone other than the author of a work product examines that product manually to find defects and improvement opportunities. An *inspection* is a type of formal and rigorous team peer review that can discover more subtle problems than individual reviewers might spot on their own. Removing errors in the requirements saves many times the cost of the inspection because of the rapidly escalating cost of remedying defects that are found later in the project.

Unfortunately, inspections and other peer reviews of requirements documents often aren't held when intended, and those that are performed don't always go well. Reviewers take only a superficial look (if they look at all), and they miss many of the major defects that lurk in the specification. Conducting an ineffective review can give the team unjustified confidence in the work product's quality.

Improving Your Requirements Reviews

This chapter presents several ways to make your requirements reviews more effective and to encourage prospective reviewers to contribute to them. For an in-depth exploration of different peer review approaches, see *Peer Reviews in Software: A Practical Guide* (Wiegers 2002a).

Educate the reviewers

Suppose someone hands you a document and asks for your input. Your instinctive approach is to begin reading at page one and see whether any problems jump out at you as you go. Maybe you're not too sure what to look for. As you continue reading, you begin to get tired and bored. Your own work backlog tugs at your conscience. So you flip through the rest of the pages, tell the author about the minor issues you found, and move on with your life. However, there's a better way.

Don't expect that reviewers will automatically know what to do. If you're an analyst who's relying on input from others to validate and verify your requirements, you need to educate your reviewers. Ideally, you can get them to take some training on how to perform peer reviews. If not, at least tell them about the purpose of reviews, the various sorts of review approaches, and what you expect of the reviewers. This is particularly important if you plan to hold inspections, which involve a more structured process than do the more familiar informal reviews.

Peer reviews are at least as much a social interaction as they are a technical practice. Asking someone to tell you what you've done wrong with your work is a learned behavior, not an instinctive behavior. Authors need to learn how to request and accept constructive input about mistakes they've made. If you're holding inspections or team reviews that involve a meeting, make sure the participants understand how to collaborate effectively and constructively. Many organizations hold ineffective reviews because participants are nervous and they aren't sure how to behave in a review meeting.

One government agency that hired me as a consultant told me that their review participants refer to the review as "going into the shark tank"—not an appealing prospect. If you've been burned by a caustic review in the past, you'll be reluctant to participate in such a stressful and ego-busting experience again. Therefore, it's important to make reviews be constructive experiences in which all participants feel that they're contributing to improving the team's collective work products.

People need to be thoughtful about how they provide feedback to the author of the work product being reviewed. I like to simply make observations about the product, rather than telling the author he did something wrong. If you're the author, you might react differently if a reviewer says, "You forgot to fill in section 3.4 of the SRS template," instead of saying, "I didn't see anything entered in section 3.4 here," or "Section 3.4 seems to be missing." Be thoughtful about how you phrase your comments. Perhaps you're a reviewer today, but you might be the author the next time.

Tell the reviewers what kind of input you're seeking in each situation so that they can focus their attention on that type of information. Give them tips on how to study and analyze a requirements specification. For example, you might invite reviewers to start reading at some point other than the beginning of the document. After all, developers won't read the entire document sequentially during construction. This is a way to get fresh eyes looking at various sections, rather than having all reviewers peter out partway through the document and miss a lot of errors in the latter pages. Some people suggest reading the document from back to front, section by section, to see whether the questions they come up with are all answered earlier in the document.

Give the reviewers a checklist of typical requirements errors so that they can focus their examination on those points. You can find checklists for reviewing software requirements specifications and use case documents at *http://www.processimpact.com/pr_goodies.shtml*. You might suggest that the reviewers make multiple passes through the document, perhaps during separate review cycles of a growing document. They can look for different types of problems from the checklist during each pass. Alternatively, ask different reviewers to use separate parts of the checklist to broaden the review coverage. Eventually requirements reviewers will internalize the review checklists and know what sorts of problems to look for.

Don't overwhelm the reviewers

Many analysts wait until their requirements specification is complete before they present it to some reviewers. Busy developers, testers, project managers, and users have difficulty finding the time to scrutinize a large document on short notice. It's far more effective to review the evolving document incrementally. Give reviewers just a few pages at a time, preferably soon after an elicitation activity. Nearly anyone should be able to spend 30 minutes reviewing a small quantity of information once in a while.

Incremental, informal reviews will uncover a lot of problems. Expect to make multiple review passes through the requirements documentation over time. Each review cycle will detect errors that the reviewers didn't spot the first time. As the requirements continue to change and grow, people might need to revisit portions of the requirements documentation that they examined in an earlier draft. Combine these sorts of informal individual reviews, which I call *peer deskchecks*, with formal inspections of documents that are nearly done.

Build a collaborative partnership with the user representatives and other project participants

Explain to users why their input is so critical to ensuring the quality of the requirements and how it contributes to the quality of the ultimate software product. Make them understand that their review effort is a vital contribution, not an idle exercise. Begin forging this collaboration early in the project so that these participants realize they're valued members of the team.

On many projects, my teams at Kodak used product champions, key customer representatives who worked closely with the requirements analysts on a project. (See Chapter 6, "The Myth of the On-Site Customer.") We negotiated the exact responsibilities with each champion. But one responsibility was *not* optional: to review requirements specifications and evaluate prototypes. Without user review, we couldn't tell whether we'd accurately captured the voice of the customer. We were pleased that all our product champions accepted this responsibility and provided great value through their reviews.

Invite the right reviewers

Determine early in the project what perspectives you need represented in your requirements reviews and who can provide these perspectives. Figure 8-1 illustrates the essential points of view a requirements review should take into account. Particularly consider getting the participation of the following:

- Customers who provided requirements input.
- Developers who will have to design and implement the requirements.
- Testers who will have to verify the proper implementation of the requirements.

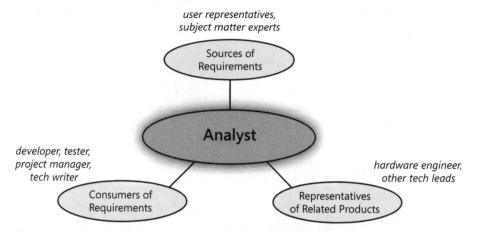

Figure 8-1   Perspectives to be represented in a requirements review.

Work products must be reviewed in context, not in isolation. The reviewers must ascertain whether the work product meets its own specification. The top-level requirements documentation has no specification or reference document, so you need customers or others who provided requirements input to review the deliverable. Also invite another analyst who's adroit at spotting poorly written or missing requirements. The downstream consumers of the requirements specification can check to see whether it will satisfy their needs. And if your product connects in some way to any other products, have representatives of those other components make sure the pieces will fit together properly.

Rather than having these different reviewers just read through the document, tell them about *perspective-based reading*, or PBR (Wiegers 2002a). In PBR, each reviewer examines the deliverable from the point of view of a specific document consumer. The customer seeks to determine whether the documented requirements would in fact let him achieve his business objectives. The developer checks to see whether the document contains the information he needs to design and implement a solution. The tester considers whether the requirements are precise and detailed enough to be verifiable. These different points of view will reveal different types of problems.

Have reviewers examine appropriate deliverables

It might not be reasonable to expect all your user representatives to effectively review a detailed SRS. They should certainly understand use cases, though, as use cases ought to be written from the user's point of view. Make sure your reviewers can comprehend the requirements documents and diagrams well enough to validate them. If the requirements documents are too technical for the reviewers to follow, you're wasting their time.

Design for reviewability

Present the information in a specification in ways that make it easy for reviewers to understand it and to examine it for problems. There are many ways to communicate besides natural language text. If your eyes glaze over when reading a long list of textual requirements, maybe a diagram or a table would be an effective alternative. (See Chapter 19, "The Six Blind Men and the Requirements.") Remember that a requirements specification is a communication tool. If your requirements deliverables don't speak to their intended audiences, the deliverables need further work.

Inspect all requirements deliverables

Informal reviews are helpful, but the more formal inspections find more defects. Inspections and other group reviews are a way to force the issue of getting reviewers to actually look at the work product. Inspections are a powerful way to spot ambiguous requirements. During an inspection, one inspector (not the author) serves as the *reader*. The reader presents his interpretation of each requirement to the other inspectors. If his interpretation doesn't match their own understanding, perhaps the team has detected an ambiguity, something that can be interpreted in more than one way. Individual informal reviews often overlook ambiguities because an ambiguous requirement can make sense to each reader even though it might mean something different to each of them.

Emphasize finding major errors

The real leverage from a review comes from finding major errors of commission and omission. These are the defects that can help you avoid extensive—and expensive—rework much later in the project. Ambiguous and erroneous requirements send developers and testers in the wrong direction. Missing requirements are among the hardest errors to detect. They're invisible, so inspectors don't see them during their individual preparation. Because they don't exist, the inspection reader won't describe them. See Chapter 7 of *Software Requirements, Second Edition* for some tips on identifying missing requirements.

Fixing typographical and grammatical errors is useful because any changes that enhance effective communication are valuable. However, this should be done before sending out the document out for broad review, perhaps by having a single skilled editor go through it initially. Otherwise, reviewers can trip on these superficial errors and fail to spot the big defects that lie underneath. When I see an issue list from a review that contains mostly cosmetic and spelling mistakes, I worry that perhaps the reviewers overlooked major problems.

No analyst can get the requirements right on his own. Get a little help from your friends to make sure that what you've written will satisfy customer needs and will let the rest of the development team do a first-class job.

Part IV
On Use Cases

I'm a strong proponent of the use case technique for exploring user requirements with suitable user representatives. Use cases shift the focus of the requirements discussion from product features to user goals. This shift in perspective greatly increases the chance of building the right set of functionality. However, I've seen many organizations struggle to implement use cases in a practical and effective fashion.

Chapter 9—"Use Cases and Scenarios and Stories, Oh My!"—distinguishes these three related usage-oriented techniques. A term often used when discussing use cases is *actor*. An actor is similar to a user, but not identical. This subtlety can be confusing; Chapter 10, "Actors and Users," sharpens the distinction.

When analysts begin employing use cases, they often attempt to fit every functionality fragment into a use case. They might discard the other requirements documentation techniques with which they're familiar and try to rely solely on use cases. This strategy doesn't work well in most situations. Use cases are valuable, but they aren't a panacea for all requirements challenges. Chapter 11, "When Use Cases Aren't Enough," describes a practical way to apply use cases to frame the discussion with users, as well as how you can derive the necessary functional requirements from use cases. The chapter also describes some types of projects for which use cases aren't terribly helpful and an alternative strategy of creating event-response tables.

Chapter 9
Use Cases and Scenarios and Stories, Oh My!

Many requirements analysts have learned that elicitation discussions that focus on users and usage generally yield the best results. A usage-centric approach to system specification is superior to the traditional emphasis on system features and functions. Most users find it more natural to talk about their business tasks and usage goals than to try to identify all the functionality they expect to see in the product. *Use cases, scenarios,* and *user stories* are terms that are used frequently when describing a system's user requirements (Alexander and Maiden 2004). These terms can be confusing. This chapter more clearly defines these terms and concepts.

Use Cases

Use cases are all the rage in requirements circles these days.[1] A use case is, literally, a case of usage. In other words, a use case is a description of a sequence of interactions between the system and one or more external actors—see Chapter 10, "Actors and Users"—that results in an outcome that provides value to at least one actor. Alistair Cockburn (2001) says that a use case "describes the system's behavior and interactions under various conditions as a response to a request on behalf of one of the stakeholders—the *primary actor*—showing how the primary actor's goal gets delivered or fails."

The name given to a use case should indicate the value the use case will deliver to an actor. By convention, a use case name always begins with a verb. The name also contains an object, which is a noun. Adjectives and adverbs are optional. Good examples of use case names are Reserve Rental Car, Print Invoice, Register for Payroll Deduction, and Check Flight Status.

---

1. I'm assuming that you already have some familiarity with use cases and the terminology associated with them: *normal flow, alternative flows, exceptions, preconditions, postconditions,* and so on. If these terms are unfamiliar, I refer you to Chapter 8 of *Software Requirements, Second Edition* (Wiegers 2003a) and to *Use Cases: Requirements in Context, Second Edition* (Kulak and Guiney 2004). Note that the terminology used in various books on use cases is not consistent, although the general principles are.

When working with users to identify use cases, I often listen for the phrase "I need to" to indicate that the user has a specific objective in mind that the system can help him achieve. While discussing a proposed car rental kiosk at an airport, for example, I might ask a user representative, "When might you use a kiosk like this?" The user might reply, "I would use it when I need to reserve a car." Parsing this response tells us that one candidate use case for the product is Reserve Rental Car. Another possible user response is, "I would use the kiosk when I need to return a car I rented." This implies a use case named Return Rental Car. Use strong, specific action verbs when naming your use cases (Kulak and Guiney 2004).

You can describe use cases at various levels of detail. Figure 9-1 suggests a template for documenting use cases. You can download this template, including guidance for completing each section, from *http://www.processimpact.com/goodies.shtml*. Fully populating the various fields in the template creates quite a rich description of the use case. However, it's not always necessary to complete the entire template. For each of your use cases, consider which of the following levels of detail is most appropriate.

Use Case ID:			
Use Case Name:			
Created By:		Last Updated By:	
Date Created:		Date Last Updated:	

Actors:	
Description:	
Trigger:	
Preconditions:	
Postconditions:	
Normal Flow:	
Alternative Flows:	
Exceptions:	
Includes:	
Priority:	
Frequency of Use:	
Business Rules:	
Special Requirements:	
Assumptions:	
Notes and Issues:	

Figure 9-1   Template for documenting a use case.

- The simplest use case specification consists of a unique identifier, a use case name, the actors involved in performing the use case, a brief textual description, and perhaps the event that triggers the use case execution. This is enough information to allow an initial prioritization of your use cases, perhaps determining which ones will be addressed in each planned product release. Prioritizing makes sure the team invests its energy working on the most timely and most important use cases.

- Most use cases will benefit from additional information. At this level, you detail the normal flow of events, showing the principal or default sequence of steps in the dialogue between actor and system that leads to the actor's goal. Specify the preconditions and postconditions for the use case, recognizing that you'll refine them as you learn more about the use case and even as the team gets into design and implementation of the use case. Also identify the alternative flows and exceptions that could take place and any pertinent business rules that affect the use case.

- A complete use case description includes the previous items plus specifics about how the system will handle the alternative flows and exceptions, as well as the remaining fields in the use case template.

You can judge what level of detail is appropriate for a given use case by considering how much information you need to communicate to users, developers, and testers. You might perform an initial use case analysis at the first level of detail and then refine each use case further as it comes into scope for a particular release iteration.

Use cases describe user requirements at a fairly high level of abstraction. Use cases should be named to encompass a set of logically related user tasks. These related user tasks constitute separate scenarios, variations on a common theme. Scenarios represent specializations of the general user goal stated in the use case name, or alternative pathways by which the user could reach that goal. If you find yourself caught in a use case explosion, with hundreds of use cases for a modest-sized system, see whether you can combine related use cases into a single, more general one. This merging involves moving the use case to a higher level of abstraction that will encompass a set of similar user tasks, thereby simplifying the requirements problem.

This past week, I had a discussion with a student in a class I was teaching on use cases. He described two use cases from his current project. One use case was Request Initial Reimbursement for Travel Expenses and the second was Request Supplemental Reimbursement for Travel Expenses. These sounded to me like two variations on a single use case. Generalizing the use case name to be Request Reimbursement for Travel Expenses could encompass both of these closely related user objectives. This avoids the need to duplicate a lot of functionality in two similar use case descriptions.

Scenarios

When dealing with user requirements, the analyst needs to operate at various levels of abstraction. As Figure 9-2 illustrates, use cases appear at the highest level of abstraction. Suppose you're exploring requirements for an application that will be used in a store that ships packages by various methods. One use case is Prepare a Mailing Label. This represents a high level of abstraction. It encompasses any possible package that any customer might want to ship by any method to any destination. You can also slide down the abstraction scale a little to a more specific situation: prepare a mailing label to send a package by second-day air via carrier X. This is an example of a scenario.

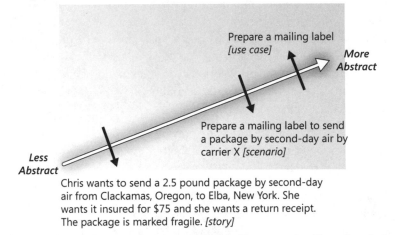

Chris wants to send a 2.5 pound package by second-day air from Clackamas, Oregon, to Elba, New York. She wants it insured for $75 and she wants a return receipt. The package is marked fragile. *[story]*

Figure 9-2   Where use cases, scenarios, and user stories fit on the abstraction scale.

We can define a *scenario* as a specific path through a use case or a specific instance of executing a use case. Each use case encompasses multiple scenarios, each of which involves certain data combinations and branches taken through the use case execution. Some scenarios result in success; that is, the user achieves his intended goal. The most typical or default scenario is called the *normal flow* of the use case. Synonyms for this scenario include the *flow of events, normal course of events, main course, basic course, basic flow, primary scenario, main success scenario,* and *happy path.*

Other pathways through the use case that also result in success are called *alternative flows* (sometimes called *extensions*). A use case can have zero, one, or many alternative flows. If a user representative in a use case workshop uses the phrase "the default should be," he's about to describe the normal flow. The phrase "but the user should also have the option to" most likely introduces an alternative flow. In the example from the previous section, the initial reimbursement for travel expenses is the normal flow, whereas supplemental reimbursement constitutes a less common alternative flow.

In addition, use cases typically identify conditions under which they might fail to complete successfully. These are called *exceptions, exception flows,* or *exception paths*. Some authors do not distinguish exceptions from alternative flows (for example, Cockburn 2001), but I find it useful to separate them. When doing release planning, you might elect to implement only the normal flow and certain alternative flows of a particular use case in the first release, deferring other alternative flows to later product releases. However, you *must* implement all the exceptions that could take place in those success flows that you do choose to implement. Therefore, I prefer to separate exceptions in the use case documentation and to identify the success flow with which each exception is associated.

Executing a particular scenario involves traversing a specific combination of flows. Figure 9-3 illustrates the various flows in a use case. The normal flow consists of a series of steps, a dialogue between the primary actor, the system, and possibly some secondary actors. (See Chapter 10, "Actors and Users.") The normal flow is shown in Figure 9-3 as a straight line that leads downward to a successful outcome. When you write the normal flow, don't worry about any branching options the actor has available or things that could go wrong. I refer to the normal flow as flow 0.

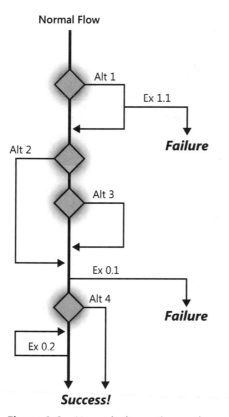

Figure 9-3   Normal, alternative, and exception flows in a use case.

We can show each alternative flow (Alt 1 through Alt 4) as branching off from the normal flow at a particular point in the actor-system dialog. Perhaps the system offers the user an option or the system encounters some condition that causes a deviation from the normal flow. These branch points are shown as diamonds in Figure 9-3; flowcharts and activity diagrams are fine ways to document these things. Many alternative flows return to the main flow at some point (Alt 1, Alt 2, Alt 3). Others, such as Alt 4, terminate successfully, perhaps with some outcome slightly different from that of the main flow.

Exceptions, such as Ex 0.1 and Ex 0.2, also branch off the main flow. Each of these branches represents some condition that has the potential to prevent a successful outcome for the use case. Sometimes the system might be able to recover from the exception, as in Ex 0.2, but other times it results in a use case failure (Ex 0.1): The primary actor does not achieve the goal stated in the use case name and described in its postconditions. Alternative flows can have their own exceptions, such as Ex 1.1 for alternative flow Alt 1.

As you can see from this structure, a use case can be quite complex. A scenario consists of a single path through the use case that involves some combination of normal and/or exception flows. Referring again to Figure 9-3, some scenarios would cover the following paths, although it's possible that not all these scenarios make sense from a business flow point of view:

Normal flow	Normal flow + Ex 0.1
Normal flow + Alt 1	Normal flow + Alt 1 + Ex 1.1
Normal flow + Alt 2	Normal flow + Alt 2 + Ex 0.2
Normal flow + Alt 1 + Alt 3	Normal flow + Alt 2 + Alt 4

You can see from Figure 9-3 that not all flow combinations are feasible. If you go down path Ex 1.1, you won't be going down Alt 2, Alt 3, Alt 4, or any other exceptions. If your scenario involves Alt 2, you'll never have the option to take Alt 3. There could be additional scenario variations that involve specific data combinations that lead to, say, performing certain calculations differently even though they all take the same flow path. This sort of scenario analysis is also valuable when identifying test cases based on requirements (Leffingwell and Widrig 2003).

User Stories

User stories have been popularized through the agile software development methodology called Extreme Programming. Agile methodologies advocate lightweight approaches to requirements engineering, project management, and other aspects of software development. Rather than developing a comprehensive set of use cases or a detailed software requirements specification, the analyst (who is often the developer) works with users to collect stories. Extreme Programming defines a story as "one thing that the customer wants the system to do" (Beck 2000). In Extreme Programming, users provide stories that the analyst concisely writes on an index card in natural language text using the business domain's terminology. The stories are elaborated and modified throughout the project based on user input. The entire story consists of this initial story card, plus all the subsequent conversations that take place regarding that story among project stakeholders and perhaps user acceptance tests.

The examples of user stories given in books on agile development cover a wide range of requirement categories and abstraction levels (for example, Beck and West 2004). They range from individual functional requirements to scenarios, use cases, product features, business objectives, constraints, quality attributes, business rules, user interface issues, and desired characteristics of the product. The analyst might break complex stories into multiple smaller stories that can be understood better, estimated better, and perhaps implemented independently. But the examples of user stories I've seen for agile development don't differentiate various types of requirements information. Anything the customer "wants the system to do" constitutes a story.

I have a problem with this definition of the term *story*. The essence of user-centric and usage-centric requirements elicitation is to *focus on what the user wants to do*, not what the user wants the system to do. Asking the latter question takes us back to the shortcomings of the original system-focused requirements exploration process. The "stories" generated in this fashion can become near-random bits of information, all churned together in the discussion between analyst and customers. They lack the usage-centered organizing structure that use cases and scenarios provide.

I think of stories somewhat differently. I consider a story to be a specific, concrete instance of a user's interaction with a system to achieve a goal. Stories lie at the low end of the abstraction scale. Earlier in this chapter, Figure 9-2 illustrated a story for a package-shipping store's new software system:

> *Chris wants to send a 2.5-pound package by second-day air from Clackamas, Oregon, to Elba, New York. She wants it insured for $75 and she wants a return receipt. The package is marked fragile.*

During user requirements development, you can take a top-down approach or a bottom-up approach. You can start at the high abstraction level by having some users identify use cases and then prioritizing them and elaborating them into further detail at the right time. A story such as the previous one provides a good starting point for a bottom-up strategy. You can say to the store's user representative, "Please tell me about the last time someone came into the store with a package to ship." The user might relate an experience similar to the one about Chris. This is a very specific instance of how a store employee might have to prepare a particular mailing label. If you don't have access to real users who can tell you stories, consider inventing stories for the user-substitute personas you've identified. (See Chapter 6, "The Myth of the On-Site Customer.")

The analyst can abstract upward to generalize that one story, or a set of similar stories or scenarios, to cover a variety of mailing label possibilities within the same use case. If you were to treat each of these specific user stories as a separate use case, you would wind up with a vast number of use cases, many of which are identical except for small variations, say in the package weight, destination, or shipping method. Such a use case explosion provides a clue that you need to climb farther up the abstraction scale.

Use cases, scenarios, and stories all provide powerful ways to hear and understand the voice of the customer. Unless you focus on the user's goals and vision, your team can easily implement a stunning set of functionality that simply doesn't let users get their jobs done in a way they find appealing. And that would be a shame.

Chapter 10
Actors and Users

Software products are created for users, be they human beings, pieces of hardware, or other software systems. A *user* is a stakeholder who will interact with a completed system either directly (that is, hands on) or indirectly (for example, using reports from the system but not generating those reports personally). Users can be grouped into *user classes*, communities of users who have similar characteristics and similar requirements for a system.

Discussions of use cases always involve the concept of actors. An *actor* is an entity outside the system boundary that interacts with the system for the purpose of completing a transaction, such as a use case. Actors are related to—but are not precisely the same as—user classes. This distinction between user classes and actors is subtle. It doesn't help that the books on use cases employ somewhat different terminology. Here are the key points:

- User classes represent groups of actual people or other types of users (hardware devices or software systems). A human user is a member of one or more user classes. You need to identify your product's user classes so that you know which people to talk with about requirements. You also need to understand which user classes are "favored" (Gause and Lawrence 1999). Satisfying the needs of a favored user class is more important from a business perspective than meeting the needs of other groups of users. This distinction helps when making priority decisions and resolving requirement conflicts.

- An actor is an abstraction, a role performed by a member of a specific user class when he interacts with a product at a specific time. When you are talking with user class representatives, have them identify the various roles that members of each class can perform from time to time. If those user roles involve interacting with the system through a use case, the roles represent actor names. Consider developing *personas*, descriptions of representative actors who can execute certain use cases. (See Chapter 6, "The Myth of the On-Site Customer.")

I think of the members of each user class as having a stack of hats available, each of which is labeled with a particular actor name. Whenever a user needs to perform a specific use case with the system, he puts on the hat labeled with the name of the actor who initiates that use case. The system thinks it's interacting with the actor, regardless of what user class that individual user belongs to.

Figure 10-1 illustrates the relationship between actors and user classes for a bank. Bank Customers constitute one class of users of banking services. A particular Bank Customer might perform various functions from time to time with the bank's software systems, perhaps as an indirect user, working through a bank employee. When performing those functions, the Bank Customer is assuming the role of a particular actor. When he makes a cash withdrawal from an automated teller machine (ATM), the customer is performing the role of an Account Owner. This is more precise than calling him a generic Bank Customer. As far as the ATM is concerned, it's performing a service for the Account Owner.

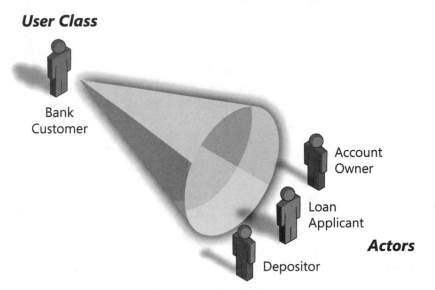

Figure 10-1   A member of one user class could take on multiple actor roles.

On another occasion, that same customer might walk into the bank and apply for a loan. At that time, he's performing the role of the Loan Applicant actor, not an account owner. The system the customer is interacting with at that time thinks of the user as being a Loan Applicant. In a third situation, a bank customer might deposit a check into an account he doesn't own, perhaps on behalf of his spouse or a business colleague. In that case, the customer is filling the role of a Depositor actor. Many actor names end in *-er* or *-or*, which indicates that the actor is a performer attempting to accomplish a particular objective.

There could also be a many-to-one relationship between user classes and actors, as Figure 10-2 illustrates. When I worked on a Chemical Tracking System project at one company, we had several important user classes: chemists, chemical technicians, members of the chemical stockroom staff, and laboratory managers. Each of these groups had largely different sets of requirements, but there was some overlap. For example, members of all these user classes might have to place requests for chemicals periodically. No one at this company had a job title of "chemical requester." The Chemical Requester actor is an abstraction that represents anybody who needs to request a chemical and is authorized to do so. The system doesn't care whether the person requesting a chemical is a chemist, a lab manager, or someone else. All the software knows is that a Chemical Requester actor is executing certain use cases associated with chemical request activities.

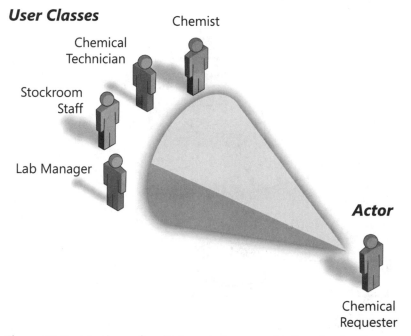

User Classes

Chemist

Chemical
Technician

Stockroom
Staff

Lab Manager

Actor

Chemical
Requester

Figure 10-2   Members of multiple user classes could all perform as the same actor.

Actors appear in use case diagrams drawn according to the convention of the Unified Modeling Language (UML) (Booch, Rumbaugh, and Jacobson 1999). Figure 10-3 shows a portion of a use case diagram for the Chemical Tracking System. The box represents the system boundary. Each oval inside the box represents a single use case, something a user would need to accomplish with the help of the system. The stick figures outside the box represent actors. The stick figure notation is used whether the actor is a human being or an inanimate entity.

An arrow drawn from an actor to a use case indicates that the actor can initiate the corresponding use case; this is the *primary actor* for that use case. The Chemical Requester actor can initiate the use cases Request a Chemical, Receive Chemical, Check Order Status, and so on. An arrow directed from a use case to an actor indicates a *secondary actor*. Secondary actors participate in the completion of a use case, but they don't derive the benefit from the use case. The primary actor gets the benefit. The Training Database and Buyer actors are secondary actors with respect to the Request a Chemical use case. The Chemical Tracking System might have to rely on the Training Database to see whether a user is properly trained in how to handle a dangerous chemical. Requests for chemicals that need to be purchased from a vendor will be routed to the Buyer for handling. Note that actors are primary or secondary with respect to a specific use case, not with respect to the entire system.

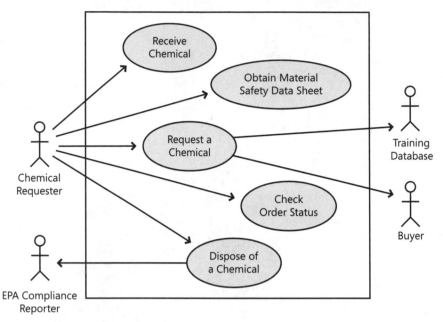

Figure 10-3   Use case diagrams show primary and secondary actors for specific use cases.

As you begin your requirements exploration, be sure to identify your user classes so that you know who you'll need to talk to in order to discover user requirements. Key representatives of user classes can work with the requirements analyst as product champions. (See Chapter 6.) The product champions identify the use cases that represent tasks or goals that members of their user class will need to accomplish with the system's help. As you explore each use case, think of an appropriate name to describe the actor who will initiate that use case. Try to select a name that reflects what the user is attempting to accomplish, such as Chemical Requester, Buyer, or Loan Applicant. Consider whether members of other user classes might also have occasion to perform that same use case–that is, whether they might have occasion to function in that same actor role. The analyst should consult representatives of those user classes to see if their stated needs enrich his understanding of the use case, perhaps by identifying additional alternative flows.

Consider developing catalogs that describe your common user classes and actors so that you can reuse these definitions in a consistent fashion across multiple projects. Any opportunities for requirements reuse will reduce errors, save time, and help you build a more cohesive set of integrated products.

Chapter 11

When Use Cases Aren't Enough

Use cases are recognized as a powerful technique for exploring user requirements. The great benefit they provide is to bring a user-centric and usage-centered perspective to requirements elicitation discussions. The analyst employs use cases to understand what the user is trying to accomplish and how he envisions his interactions with the product leading to the intended user value. Putting the user at the center is much better than focusing on product features, menus, screens, and functions that characterize traditional requirements discussions. And the structure that use cases provide is far superior to the nearly worthless technique of asking users, "What do you want?" or "What are your requirements?"

As with most new software development techniques, use cases have acquired a bit of a mystique, some misconceptions, overblown hype, and polarized camps of enthusiasts who will all try to teach you the One True Use Case Way. In this chapter, I share my perspectives on when use cases work well, when they don't, and what to do when use cases aren't a sufficient solution to the requirements problem.

The Power of Use Cases

I'm a strong believer in the use case approach. Use cases are an excellent way to structure the dialogue with users about the goals they need to accomplish with the help of the system. Users can relate to and review use cases because the analyst writes them from the user's point of view, describing aspects of the user's business. In my experience, once they get past the discomfort of trying a new technique, users readily accept the use case method as a way to explore requirements.

I'm often asked how to write requirements specifications so that users can read and understand them and also so that they contain all the detail that developers need. In many cases, one requirements representation won't meet both of these objectives. Users can comprehend use cases, but they might balk at reviewing a more detailed functional requirements specification. Use cases give developers an overall understanding of the system's behavior that fragments of individual functionality cannot. However, developers usually need considerably more information than use cases provide so that they know just what to build. In many circumstances, the combination of employing use cases to represent user requirements and a software requirements specification to contain functional and nonfunctional requirements meets both sets of needs.

Project Type Limitations

My experience has shown that use cases are an effective technique for many, but not all, types of projects. Use cases focus on the user's interactions with the system to achieve a valuable outcome. Therefore, use cases work great for interactive end-user applications, including Web sites. They're also useful for kiosks and other types of devices with which users interact.

However, use cases are less valuable for projects involving data warehouses, batch processes, hardware products with embedded control software, and computationally intensive applications. In these sorts of systems, the deep complexity doesn't lie in the user-system interactions. It might be worthwhile to identify use cases for such a product, but use case analysis will fall short as a technique for defining all the system's behavior.

 I once worked on a computational program that modeled the behavior of a multi-stage photographic system. This software used a Monte Carlo statistical simulation to perform many complex calculations and it presented the results graphically to the user. The user-system dialog needed to set up each simulation run was quite simple. (I know this because I built the user interface.) The complexity resided behind the scenes, in the computational algorithms used and the reporting of results. Use cases aren't very helpful for eliciting the requirements for these aspects of a system.

Use cases have limitations for systems that involve complex business rules to make decisions or perform calculations. Consider an airline flight reservation system, one of the classic examples used to illustrate use cases. Use cases are a fine technique for exploring the interactions between the traveler and the reservation system to describe the intended journey and the parameters associated with it. But when it comes to calculating the fare for a specific flight itinerary, a use case discussion won't help. Such calculations are driven by the interaction of highly complex business rules, not by how the user imagines conversing with the system.

Nor are use cases the best technique for understanding certain real-time systems that involve both hardware and software components. Think about a complex highway intersection. It includes sensors in the road to detect cars, traffic signals, buttons pedestrians can press to cross the street, pedestrian walk signals, and so forth. Use cases don't make much sense for specifying a system of this nature. Here are some possible use cases for a highway intersection:

- A driver wants to go through the intersection.
- A driver wants to turn left when coming from a particular direction.
- A pedestrian wants to cross one of the streets.

These approximate use cases, but they aren't very illuminating. Exploring the interactions between these actors (drivers and pedestrians) and the intersection-control software system just scratches the surface of what's happening with the intersection. The use cases don't provide nearly enough information for the analyst to define the functionality for the intersection-control software.

Use cases aren't particularly helpful for specifying the requirements for batch processes or time-triggered functions, either. My local public library's information system automatically sends me an e-mail to remind me when an item I've borrowed is due back soon. This e-mail is generated by a scheduled process that checks the status of borrowed items during the night (the one I received today was sent at 1:06 AM) and sends out notifications. Some analysts regard "time" to be an actor so that they can structure this system behavior in the form of a use case. I don't find that helpful, though. If you know the system needs to perform a time-triggered function, just write the functional requirements for that function, instead of packaging it into a contrived use case.

Event-Response Tables

A more effective technique for identifying requirements for certain types of systems is to consider the external events the system must detect. Depending on the state of the system at the time a given event is detected, the system produces a particular response. Event-response tables are a convenient way to collect this information (Wiegers 2003a). Events could be signals received from sensors, time-based triggers (such as scheduled program executions), or user actions that cause the system to respond in some way. Event-response tables are related to use cases. In fact, the trigger that initiates a use case is sometimes termed a *business event*.

The highway intersection system described earlier has to deal with various events, including these:

- A sensor detects a car approaching in one of the through lanes.
- A sensor detects a car approaching in a left-turn lane.
- A pedestrian presses a button to request to cross a street.
- One of many timers counts down to zero.

Exactly what happens in response to an external event depends on the state of the system at the time it detects the event. The system might initiate a timer to prepare to change a light from green to amber and then to red. The system might activate a Walk sign for a pedestrian (if the sign currently reads Don't Walk), or change it to a flashing Don't Walk (if the sign currently says Walk), or change it to a solid Don't Walk (if it's currently flashing). The analyst needs to write the functional requirements to specify ways to detect the events and the decision logic involved in combining events with states to produce system behaviors. Table 11-1 presents a fragment of what an event-response table might look like for such a system. Each expected system behavior consists of a combination of event, system state, and response.

State-transition diagrams and statechart diagrams are other ways to represent this information at a higher level of abstraction. Use cases just aren't enormously helpful in this situation.

Table 11-1 Partial Event-Response Table for a Highway Intersection

Event	System State	Response
Road sensor detects vehicle entering left-turn lane.	Left-turn signal is red. Cross-traffic signal is green.	Start green-to-amber countdown timer for cross-traffic signal.
Green-to-amber countdown timer reaches zero.	Cross-traffic signal is green.	1. Turn cross-traffic signal amber. 2. Start amber-to-red countdown timer.
Amber-to-red countdown timer reaches zero.	Cross-traffic signal is amber.	1. Turn cross-traffic signal red. 2. Wait 1 second. 3. Turn left-turn signal green. 4. Start left-turn-signal countdown timer.
Pedestrian presses a specific walk-request button.	Pedestrian sign is solid Don't Walk. Walk-request countdown timer is not activated.	Start walk-request countdown timer.
Pedestrian presses walk-request button.	Pedestrian sign is solid Don't Walk. Walk-request countdown timer is activated.	Do nothing.
Walk-request countdown timer reaches zero plus the amber display time.	Pedestrian sign is solid Don't Walk.	Change all green traffic signals to amber.
Walk-request countdown timer reaches zero.	Pedestrian sign is solid Don't Walk.	1. Change all amber traffic signals to red. 2. Wait 1 second. 3. Set pedestrian sign to Walk. 4. Start don't-walk countdown timer.

Here's another type of project for which use cases aren't sufficient. I enjoy watching auto races, probably because I raced stock cars myself (alas, with little success) as a teenager. Several shopping malls throughout the United States have NASCAR race-car simulators. These consist of small car bodies mounted on motion-control bases. The customer is a driver in a computer-controlled simulated race. Each driver's view of the racetrack is projected on a screen in front of his car. The driver is racing against whatever other customers happen to be competing in that race as well as against several simulated drivers that the computer controls. The car body tilts and sways on its motion-control base during the race in response to the driver's actions. A synthesized voice provides information to the driver over a speaker, warning when other cars are nearby and reporting the driver's position and how many laps are left in the race. It's a blast!

Defining the requirements for this complex system of interacting hardware and software components demands more than use cases. There aren't that many use cases for the driver. He can press the accelerator and the brake pedal, turn the steering wheel, and shift gears, but these aren't truly use cases—they're events. A great deal of the product's complexity lies not in the user interactions but under the hood (literally, in this case). An event-response approach will go much farther toward understanding the requirements for this kind of system. So although use cases are valuable for systems in which much of the complexity lies in the interactions between the user and the computer, they are not effective for some other types of products.

Use Cases Don't Replace Functional Requirements

One book about use cases states, "To sum up, all functional requirements can be captured as use cases, and many of the nonfunctional requirements can be associated with use cases" (Bittner and Spence 2003). I agree with the second part of this sentence but not with the first part. It is certainly true that use cases are a powerful technique for discovering the functional requirements for a system being developed. However, this statement suggests that use cases are the only tool needed for representing a software system's functionality.

This notion that all functional requirements can fit into a set of use cases and that use cases contain all the functional requirements for a system appears in many of the books and methodologies that deal with use cases. The thinking seems to be that the use cases *are* the functional requirements. If the analyst writes good use cases, the developers are supposed to be able to build the system from that information, along with nonfunctional requirements information that's included in a supplementary specification.[1] Nonfunctional requirements, such as performance, usability, security, and availability goals, typically relate to a specific use case or even to a particular flow within a use case.

Unfortunately, despite the thousands of students I've taught in requirements seminars over the years, I have yet to meet a single person who has found this pure use case approach to work! Perhaps some people have successfully done it, but I haven't met any of them. On the contrary, dozens of requirements analysts have told me, "We gave our use cases to the developers and they got the general idea, but the use cases just didn't contain enough information. The developers had to keep asking questions to get the additional requirements that weren't in the use cases." I suppose you could argue that they must not have been very good use cases. But when dozens of people report the same unsatisfactory experience when trying to apply a particular methodology, I question the methodology's practicality.

---

1. There's an interesting conflict in the current use case literature. Bittner and Spence (2003) provide the following definition for *supplementary requirements*: "Functional or nonfunctional requirements that are traceable to a particular use case are said to *supplement* the use case description" (their italics). However, the Unified Software Development Process, which is heavily use case driven, offers a definition of *supplementary requirement* that is directly contradictory: "A generic requirement that cannot be connected to a particular use case..." (Jacobson, Booch, and Rumbaugh 1999). It's no wonder practitioners get confused. It's generally agreed that a supplemental specification is needed to contain at the very least those nonfunctional requirements that the use cases do not describe.

There are three problems with adhering to this philosophy of use case purity. First, your use cases must contain all the functional detail that the analysts need to convey to the developers. That requires writing highly detailed use cases. The sample use cases in some books do include some complex examples. But elaborate use cases become hard to read, review, and understand.

The second problem with this approach is that it forces you to invent use cases to hold all the functional requirements because a use case is the only container you have available to describe system functionality. However, some system functionality does not fit appropriately into a use case. I have seen many new use case practitioners struggle to create inappropriate use cases to hold all the bits of functionality, to no useful end.

Logging in to an ATM or a Web site is an example that illustrates this problem. Bittner and Spence (2003) provide this good definition of use case:

> *Describes how an actor uses a system to achieve a goal and what the system does for the actor to achieve that goal. It tells the story of how the system and its actors collaborate to deliver something of value for at least one of the actors.*

By this definition, logging in to a system is not a legitimate use case because it provides no value to the person who is logging in. No one logs in to a system and feels as though he accomplished something as a result. Logging in is a means to an end, a necessary step to being able to perform use cases that do provide value. Nevertheless, the functionality to permit login and everything associated with it (such as business rules or integrity requirements regarding passwords) must be defined somewhere. If you're using only use cases to capture functional requirements, you wind up inventing artificial use cases—those that don't provide user value— just to have a place to store certain chunks of functionality. This artificiality does not add value to the requirements development process.

A third shortcoming of the use case–only philosophy is that use cases are organized in a way that makes good sense to users but not to developers. As Figure 11-1 illustrates, a use case consists of multiple small packages of information. A typical use case template contains sections for preconditions, postconditions, the normal flow of events, zero or more alternative flows (labeled with *Alt.* in Figure 11-1), zero or more exceptions (labeled with *Ex.*), possibly some business rules, and perhaps some additional special requirements.

These small packages are easy to understand and review, but they make it hard for the developer to see how the pieces fit together. As a developer, I find it more informative to see all the related requirements grouped together in a logical sequence. Suppose I read a functional requirement that implements a step in the normal flow. I want to see the requirements dealing with branch points into alternative flows and conditions that could trigger exceptions immediately following that one functional requirement. I'd like to see the requirements that handle each business rule in context, juxtaposed with the relevant system functionality.

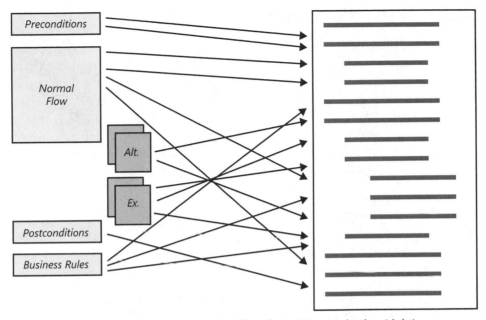

Figure 11-1 Use case organization (left) differs from SRS organization (right).

As Figure 11-1 illustrates, the functional requirements that come from the various chunks of a use case can be sprinkled throughout a hierarchically organized SRS. Traceability analysis becomes important so that you can make sure every functional requirement associated with the use case traces back to a specific part of the use case. You also want to ensure that every piece of information in the use case leads to the necessary functionality in the SRS. In short, the way a use case is organized is different from the way many developers prefer to work.

It gets even more confusing if you're employing use cases to describe the bulk of the functionality but have placed additional functional requirements that don't relate to specific use cases into a supplemental specification (Leffingwell and Widrig 2003). This approach forces the developer to get some information from the use case documentation and then to scour the supplemental specification for other relevant inputs. Before your analysts impose a particular requirements-packaging strategy on the developers, have these two groups work together to determine the most effective ways to communicate requirements information. (See Chapter 12, "Bridging Documents.")

My preference is for the analyst to create an SRS as the ultimate deliverable for the developers and testers. This SRS should contain all the known functional and nonfunctional requirements, regardless of whether they came from use cases or other sources. Functional requirements that originated in use cases should be traced back to those use cases so that readers and analysts know where they came from.

Use Cases Reveal Functional Requirements

Rather than expecting use cases to contain 100 percent of the system's functionality, I prefer to employ use cases to help the analyst discover the functional requirements. That is, the use cases become a tool rather than being an end unto themselves. Users can review the use cases to validate whether a system that implemented the use cases would meet their needs. The analyst can study each use case and derive the functional requirements the developer must implement to realize the use case in software. I like to store those functional requirements in a traditional SRS, although you could add them to the use case description if you prefer.

I'm often asked, "Which comes first: use cases or functional requirements?" The answer is use cases. Use cases represent requirements at a higher level of abstraction than do the detailed functional requirements. I like to focus initially on understanding the user's goals so that we can see how they might use the product to achieve those goals. From that information, the analyst can derive the necessary functionality that must be implemented so that the users can perform those use cases and achieve their goals.

Functional requirements—or hints about them—lurk in various parts of the use case. The remainder of this chapter describes a thought process an analyst can go through to identify the less obvious functional requirements from the elements of a use case description.

Preconditions

Preconditions state conditions that must be true before the actor can perform the use case. The system must test whether each precondition is true. However, use case descriptions rarely state what the system should do if a precondition is *not* satisfied. The analyst needs to determine how best to handle these situations.

Suppose a precondition for one use case states, "The patron's account must be set up for payroll deduction." How does the system behave if the patron attempts to perform this use case but his account is not yet set up for payroll deduction? Should the system notify the patron that he can't proceed? Or should the system perhaps give the patron the opportunity to register for payroll deduction and then proceed with the use case? Someone has to answer these questions and the SRS is the place to provide the answers.

Postconditions

Postconditions describe outcomes that are true at the successful conclusion of the use case. The steps in the normal flow naturally lead to certain postconditions that indicate the user's goal has been achieved. Other conditions, however, might not be visible to the user and therefore might not become a part of a user-centric use case description.

Consider an automated teller machine. After a cash withdrawal, the ATM software needs to update its record of the amount of cash remaining in the machine by subtracting the amount withdrawn. Perhaps if the cash remaining drops below a predetermined threshold the system is supposed to notify someone in the bank to reload the machine with additional money. I doubt any user will ever convey this information during a discussion of user requirements, yet the developer needs to know about this functionality.

How can you best communicate this knowledge to the developers and testers? There are two options. One is to leave the use case at the higher level of abstraction that represents the user's view and have the requirements analyst derive the additional requirements through analysis. The analyst can place those requirements in an SRS that is organized to best meet the developer's needs. The second alternative is for the analyst to include those additional details directly in the use case description. That behind-the-scenes information is not part of the user's view of the system as a black box. Instead, you can think of that information as being white-box details about the internal workings of the use case that the analyst must convey to the developer.

Normal and Alternative Flows

The functionality needed to carry out the dialogue between the actor and the system is usually straightforward. Simply reiterating these steps in the form of functional requirements doesn't add knowledge, although it might help organize the information more usefully for the developer. The analyst needs to look carefully at the normal flow and alternative flows to see if there's any additional functionality that isn't explicitly stated in the use case description. For example, under what conditions should the system offer the user the option to branch down an alternative flow path? Also, does the system need to do anything to reset itself so that it's ready for the next transaction after the normal flow or an alternative flow is fully executed?

Exceptions

The analyst needs to determine how the system could detect each exception and what it should do in each case. A recovery option might exist, such as asking the user to correct an erroneous data entry. If recovery isn't possible, the system might need to restore itself to the state that existed prior to beginning the use case and log the error. The analyst needs to identify the functionality associated with such recovery and restore activities and communicate that information to the developer.

Business Rules

Many use cases are influenced by business rules. The use case description should indicate which business rules pertain. It's up to the analyst to determine exactly what functionality the developer must implement to comply with each rule or to enforce it. These derived functional requirements should be recorded somewhere (I recommend documenting them in the SRS), rather than just expecting every developer to figure out the right way to comply with the pertinent business rules.

Special Requirements and Assumptions

The use case might assume that, for instance, the product's connection to the Internet is working. But what if it's not? The developer must implement some functionality to test for this error condition and handle it in an appropriate way.

In my experience, the process of having the analyst examine a use case in this fashion to derive pertinent functional requirements adds considerable value to the requirements development process. There's always more functionality hinted at in the use case than is obvious from simply reading it. Someone needs to discern this latent functionality. I would prefer to have an analyst do it rather than a developer. If your developers are sufficiently skilled at requirements analysis they could carry out this task, but they might not view it as part of their responsibilities.

I recently spoke to a highly experienced developer who said it was much more helpful to receive requirements information organized in a structured way from the analyst than to have to figure out those details on his own. This developer preferred to rely on the analyst's greater experience with understanding the problem domain and deriving the pertinent functional requirements. Not only did this result in better requirements, but it also allowed the developer to focus his talents and energy where he added the most value—in designing and coding the software.

My philosophy of employing use cases as a tool to help me discover functional requirements means that I don't feel a need to force every bit of functionality into a use case. It also gives me the option of writing use cases at whatever level of detail is appropriate. I might write some use cases in considerable detail to elaborate all their alternative flows, exceptions, and special requirements. I could leave other use cases at a high level, containing just enough information for me to deduce the pertinent functional requirements on my own. That is, I view use cases as a means to an end. The functional requirements are that "end," regardless of where you choose to store them or whether you even write them down at all.

Deriving functional requirements from the use case always takes place on the journey from ideas to executable software. The question is simply a matter of who you want to have doing that derivation and when. (See Chapter 13, "How Much Detail Do You Need?") If you deliver only use cases without all the functional detail to developers, each developer must derive the additional functionality on his own. A developer with little requirements analysis expertise might overlook some of these requirements. It's also unlikely that all developers will record the functional requirements they identify. This makes it hard for testers to know exactly what they need to test. It also increases the chance that someone will inadvertently fail to implement certain necessary functionality. If you're outsourcing construction of the software, you can't expect the vendor's developers to accurately determine the unstated functionality from a use case description.

You will almost always have additional functional requirements that do not fit nicely into a particular use case. Earlier in this chapter, I mentioned the example of logging in to a system.

Clearly, that functionality must be implemented, but I don't consider it to be a use case. You might also have functional requirements that span multiple use cases. Consider the behavior the system should exhibit if a required connection to the Internet goes down. The Internet connection could fail while the user is executing any use case. Therefore, this error condition doesn't constitute an exception flow associated with a specific use case. It needs to be detected and handled in multiple operations. The analyst can place all the functional requirements that are not associated with or derived from a particular use case into the logically appropriate section of the SRS.

As an alternative to creating separate use case and SRS documents, you could select use cases as the organizing structure for the bulk of the functional requirements in the SRS. IEEE (Institute of Electrical and Electronics Engineers) Standard 830-1998, "IEEE Recommended Practice for Software Requirements Specifications," provides guidance on how to create an SRS (IEEE 1998). According to this standard, you might organize the functional requirements by system mode, user class, objects, feature, stimulus (or external event), response, or functional hierarchy. You could also combine or nest these organizing schemes. You might have functional requirements grouped by stimulus within user class, for example. There is no universally optimal way to organize your functional requirements. Remember that the paramount objective is clear communication to all stakeholders who need to understand the requirements.

I have found use cases to be a highly valuable technique for exploring requirements on many types of projects. But I also value the structured software requirements specification as an effective place to adequately document the functional requirements. Keep in mind that these documents are simply containers for different types of requirements information. You can just as readily store use cases, functional requirements, and other types of requirements information in the database of a requirements management tool. Just don't expect use cases to replace all your other strategies for discovering and documenting software requirements.

Part V
On Writing Requirements

The heart of requirements development is to record the diverse types of requirements information in a shareable form that is as complete and precise as necessary to ensure that all project stakeholders get what they need. There's no formulaic way to do this, and there's no substitute for experience. Part V presents much practical guidance regarding the actual writing of requirements.

Chapter 12, "Bridging Documents," points out that documents that connect the work that multiple project participants do should be written from the perspective of the consumers of the document, not its author. In addition, I'm often asked how detailed the requirements need to be. Chapter 13—"How Much Detail Do You Need?"—identifies some of the factors that indicate you need more detail or can get by with defining the requirements at a higher level. Chapter 14, "To Duplicate or Not To Duplicate," addresses the thorny issue of whether you should replicate information that logically belongs in multiple places in your requirements documentation.

Chapter 15, "Elements of Requirements Style," gets down to the nuts and bolts of writing requirements. It presents several appropriate styles of writing functional requirements. It also discusses various sources of requirements ambiguity and ways to avoid them. The final chapter of Part V, "The Fuzzy Line Between Requirements and Design," looks at the gray area between these two domains. It offers suggestions for spotting both appropriate and unnecessary solutions embedded in the requirements.

Chapter 12
Bridging Documents

It's not unusual for a well-meaning requirements analyst to prepare a software requirements specification carefully and deliver it to the development team and the testers, only to have the recipients gripe about it. Here are some typical complaints:

- "This doesn't contain enough detail. Now I have to do the analyst's job to chase down this information. Either that, or I have to make my best guess."

- "There's too much detail in the requirements. I didn't need all this information, just a general idea. I already know what to build. I don't even have time to read it. In fact, I don't think I will."

- "This document contains too much design information. The analyst is trying to do the design job I'm supposed to do. These so-called 'requirements' have eliminated my creative options."

- "This document isn't organized in a way that makes sense to me. I can't find the information I need."

- "There's a lot of text in here, but I have a hard time figuring out exactly what the requirements are. I have to wade through all the descriptive text and background information in each big paragraph and hope I'm interpreting the requirement itself correctly. I can't even tell just how many requirements there are."

Software project team members create various *bridging documents*, such as an SRS. These documents communicate information to other people so that they can perform their part of the project work. That is, these documents serve as a bridge between the work one community does and the work performed by another group.

The authors of these bridging documents typically write them from their own points of view. In good faith, the author selects the information to include, and he writes and organizes it in a way that makes sense from his perspective. But that isn't necessarily the same way that will make the most sense from the *reader's* perspective. That's why, when the SRS flies over the wall from the requirements analyst and lands on the developer's head, people sometimes are unhappy.

I think we should write each bridging document from the perspective of the document *consumers*—the downstream users of the document—rather than from the author's point of view. The requirements analyst should work with developers, testers, project managers, and others who will have to use the specification to determine how best to write and structure it. The consumers of the document are an important source of input regarding what information to include, how to organize it, writing style, and the appropriate level of detail. Working together to define the document's structure and contents reflects a collaborative approach to requirements development.

 I encountered a bridging document problem recently at a telephone company I was working with. This organization has many business analysts who create requirements specifications that they hand off to the system architects on their projects. An architect complained to me that the SRS documents he received didn't always meet his needs well. Sometimes, it seemed as though the business analyst had done a lot of the high-level design already, which the architect considered as being his responsibility. In other situations, the requirements were primarily written at the user requirements level. The architect then had to derive the necessary functional requirements himself. He regarded this as being the analyst's responsibility, not his.

This is a classic situation in which the architects and business analysts need to sit down together and agree on just what information should go into the SRS. The business analysts at this organization were doing their best to supply the information they thought the architects needed at the right level of detail. Some additional input from the architects to guide the analysts' efforts would go a long way toward ensuring that future specifications properly bridge the gap between requirements development and software design.

In this book, I'm advocating a user-centric and usage-centric perspective to developing requirements specifications. Experience has taught me that looking at software systems from the perspective of the user, rather than from that of the designer, leads to superior results. The same is true of an SRS and other bridging documents. By having the work product's consumers think about how they will use those documents and what information they need to do a good job, the authors and consumers can agree on templates and conventions for producing such documents. For instance, designers or testers might find it valuable to have certain information presented visually, rather than in the form of natural language text, which probably would be the analyst's initial inclination.

Note that I'm not suggesting you create *more* requirements documentation. I'm merely proposing that the analysts, developers, and other stakeholders put their heads together to decide how best to prepare the requirements specifications they do create. Focusing on the appropriate contents like this can actually lead to shorter documents because the authors have a clearer understanding of what to include and what to leave out. The same principle of agreeing on form and contents applies to design documents, project plans, and other project deliverables that are targeted at specific readers.

Rule number one for any author is "know your audience." This applies to software project documents as well as to any other type of writing.

Chapter 13

How Much Detail Do You Need?

Requirements analysts often wonder how detailed their requirements need to be. There's no single correct answer to this question, even assuming we could agree on just exactly how to measure requirements "detail." I can give you some ways to think about how much detail is appropriate in a given situation, though.

Who Makes the Call?

The central question to consider when deciding how detailed to make the requirements is: *Who do you want to have making decisions about requirements details and when?* If you're willing to defer many of the ultimate decisions about product capabilities and characteristics to the developers, you don't need to include as much information in the requirements documentation. However, if you want to describe exactly what you expect to be delivered, more complete specifications are necessary. You need to balance cost and risk. It costs more to develop requirements in greater detail than to leave them more general. Choosing the appropriate amount of detail to include depends upon the risk associated with leaving decisions about specifics to developers.

 Let me give you an illustration about requirements detail. My house has a security alarm system. To disarm the system, I enter my passcode on a numeric keypad. At one level, we could state a requirement for this function quite simply: "When the alarm system is armed and a sensor is triggered, the user shall be able to enter a numeric passcode to disarm the system." This statement conveys the general intent, but it isn't enough information for the developer to know just what to design and build. Here are some questions that arise when considering the implications of this functional requirement:

- What are the minimum and maximum numbers of digits allowed in a passcode?

- How should the system conclude that the user has finished entering the passcode so that it can evaluate the passcode? Or should the user somehow indicate that the passcode has been fully entered so as to trigger passcode evaluation?

- How can the homeowner set and change his passcode? Is there a default?

- How long does the system wait for the user to enter the correct passcode before it sounds the alarm?

- What does the system do if the user enters an incorrect passcode before the timer runs out?

- How many entry attempts does the user get? Or perhaps it's a function of time: Can the user make as many attempts as he likes within a fixed time interval?

- If the user enters the wrong passcode, does the timer reset to zero or does the countdown continue toward sounding the alarm?

- What does the system do if the user does, or does not, enter the correct passcode within the specified time interval?

Clearly, someone has to answer these questions. If the analyst doesn't supply this sort of high-resolution information in the SRS, responsibility falls to the developer to identify all the pertinent questions and either track down the answers or make decisions based on his own judgment. Every analyst needs to decide whether he wants the developer to come up with answers for such questions on the fly at design and construction time, or whether he'd rather have customers and subject matter experts record the necessary information in the requirements specification.

Customers sometimes balk at taking the time needed to think through these kinds of issues carefully and make decisions. My response to this hesitation is to ask the customer, "If you don't want to make these decisions now, who do you think should make them and when?" Developers sometimes are comfortable with vague and incomplete specifications because it gives them the opportunity to interpret the requirements in whatever way they want at the moment. However, remember Cosmic Truth #9 from Chapter 2: "The requirements might be vague, but the product will be specific." The central issue is who the specificity comes from. Figure 13-1 identifies some situations in which you need more detail in the requirements documentation and other cases where less rigor will suffice.

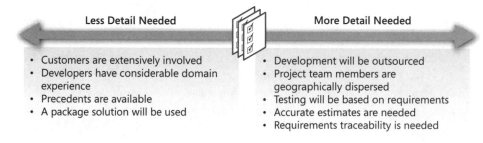

Less Detail Needed

More Detail Needed

- Customers are extensively involved
- Developers have considerable domain experience
- Precedents are available
- A package solution will be used

- Development will be outsourced
- Project team members are geographically dispersed
- Testing will be based on requirements
- Accurate estimates are needed
- Requirements traceability is needed

Figure 13-1   Some factors that influence how much requirements detail is needed.

When More Detail Is Needed

There are several situations in which writing only high-level requirements information increases the project's risk. When you encounter situations such as the following, expect to spend more time than average developing detailed requirements specifications.

Development will be outsourced.   Any time you outsource software construction rather than performing it in house, your project will benefit from comprehensive requirements documentation. When the developers are a continent or an ocean away, you don't have the opportunity for the day-to-day interactions needed to flesh out the details, answer questions, and resolve ambiguities. In certain cultures, developers will implement precisely what is specified, even if it's not complete or sensible. Without having many opportunities for clarification, you have no choice but to supply all the necessary information in the form of written specifications, designs, and acceptance test cases. Do your best to remove uncertainties before sending the specification out for implementation.

 Project team members are geographically dispersed.   It takes surprisingly little separation between project participants to inhibit communication. I learned this once when I was writing programs for a research scientist who sat just a few feet from my desk. One day he moved to a new office about a hundred feet away. My productivity dropped immediately. It now took longer to get my questions answered. I had to set up a meeting, phone him, or walk down the hall and hope to catch him, whereas previously I just had to call out my question to get an immediate response. If you're concerned about the availability of customer representatives to supply the missing details during design and construction, you'd better produce that information during requirements development.

 On another project more than 20 years ago, the three of us collaborating on a project worked in two different buildings. We didn't have a written requirements specification. Instead, we held a weekly meeting to focus our efforts for the next week, and then we went off and did our own parts of the work with limited interaction. On at least two occasions, one developer wasted a full week of effort because we walked out of our meeting with different understandings of what we were supposed to do that week. Even a limited SRS will reduce this sort of waste.

Testing will be based on requirements.   If testers will be writing comprehensive system tests or user acceptance tests from the requirements, they must know just how the system is supposed to behave under various circumstances. In fact, the concept of "testable requirements" has been proposed as a measure of software size (Wilson 1995). (See Chapter 5, "Estimating Based on Requirements.")

Tests should cover not only the expected behavior but also the known exception or error conditions that can arise. Therefore, the requirements specifications need to describe these exceptions well enough so that testers can determine whether the software is functioning correctly. You won't think of all the possible exceptions, but identifying potential problems and specifying how to handle them leads to a more robust product.

Accurate estimates are needed.   Project managers or developers who must generate effort and schedule estimates from requirements need enough detail to understand what they're getting into. I once saw an innocent-looking "functional requirement" that stated: "The editor shall respond to editing directives entered by voice." The way the SRS was written gave no hint that this one item was profoundly more complex than the other 700 functional requirements in the document. It's difficult to estimate the cost of implementation without decomposing that high-level statement into enough detail to get a good handle on its size, complexity, and difficulty.

Requirements traceability is needed.   Requirements tracing is the act of creating logical links between individual functional requirements, their origins (such as use cases, product features, or business rules), and the work products that are created to satisfy each requirement. Such downstream work products include design elements, source code modules, test cases, help screens, and documentation. If requirements tracing is important to your project, you need to specify the requirements in detail.

Evidence of requirements traceability is needed for certain safety-critical products, such as those that require U.S. Food and Drug Administration or Federal Aviation Administration (FAA) certification. For instance, the FAA's safety standard DO-178B specifies that "every line of code be directly traceable to a requirement and a test routine, and that no extraneous code outside of this process be included in the build" (from *http://www.validatedsoftware.com/ certification/certification_faq.html*). That is, traceability information ensures that your system has no orphan code and no overlooked requirements. Requirements traceability confirms that following conditions are met:

- All requirements trace forward to elements of the software design.
- Each design element can be traced back to specific requirements.
- All code written traces back to a design element and hence to a requirement.
- All requirements are implemented in the code.
- Test cases exist for each requirement.
- All test cases trace to at least one requirement.

When Less Detail Is Appropriate

It's appropriate to leave the requirements descriptions at a higher level of abstraction under several circumstances. Recognize that these are broad guidelines. Perform a risk-benefit analysis to balance the potential downside of omitting important information against the effort required to include it.

Customers are extensively involved.   If you have extensive, ongoing, and intimate involvement by the right customer representatives, you can get away with less written documentation. This is the premise behind having the on-site customer in the agile software development methodologies. (See Chapter 6, "The Myth of the On-Site Customer.") In such situations, developers need just enough written information about requirements to judge their size and to get a general idea of the customer's intent. The details come from conversations with customer representatives and subject matter experts.

This approach works only when developers have ready access to customers who have the time, knowledge, and authority to make decisions on behalf of the communities they represent. Even if the customers can provide just-in-time details, it's doubtful that anyone will record those details. This makes it harder to reach a shared expectation among the various stakeholders. Your project will have little documentation to review. You will lack a written reference to ensure that the product is adequately tested and that no requirements were inadvertently overlooked during implementation. Of course, it *is* possible to capture the detailed information as the developers obtain it, thereby growing the requirements specification (or, in some agile approaches, the test documentation) incrementally, provided someone accepts responsibility for this role.

Developers have considerable domain experience.   Developers who have extensive application domain knowledge can sometimes supply a lot of the necessary requirements details. Watch out for developers who are overconfident, certain that they understand what users need without asking. Ideally, knowledgeable representatives of specific user classes will work with the requirements analyst to develop requirements. (See Chapter 6.) There's always a risk of a disconnect when using surrogates who will not actually use the product being developed. Technologically sophisticated developers might not be representative of the typical end user. Even highly experienced developers sometimes aren't aware of the current needs in a changing business environment. If their knowledge is obsolete, they can't do a good job of supplying the missing requirements.

It's a good idea to have developers run their thoughts about requirements details past the analyst and some customer representatives before implementing them. This provides a check to make sure the fleshing out is done appropriately.

Precedents are available.   When precedents are available to use as a model, you don't need to include all the requirements details in the specification. The developers can turn to the existing product or documentation as a reference for details that aren't provided in the current specification. This might be the case when reengineering a legacy application, for example.

Watch out, though. Most software contains extensive functionality that is not immediately visible to someone who is simply looking at the user interface or a high-level product description. Some examples are exception handlers, business rule enforcement, and relationships between data in fields on a form or dialog box. You don't want every developer to reverse-engineer the existing product to figure out just what it does, possibly arriving at different conclusions.

A package solution will be used.   Projects that will be acquiring a commercial package solution for all or part of their needs don't need highly detailed requirements. There's no point in writing comprehensive functional requirements because the package vendor has already done that (or so you hope). However, it's rare that a package will fully meet your needs, so you still must specify the requirements for package extensions, integrations, and customizations.

Use cases work well for package-solution projects. The package needs to let your users accomplish specific tasks (use cases), although the details of how this works will vary from package to package (functional requirements and design). User acceptance tests based on use cases are also helpful for evaluating packages. Knowledge of the pertinent business rules is critical. The package you select must enforce the necessary business rules and let you change or customize them as necessary. Defining quality attribute requirements will also help the stakeholders choose the right package.

Implied Requirements

No requirements specification can ever fully describe a product. Nor should you ever expect written documentation to replace human dialogue. Still, I get nervous when I hear people talk about "implied" or "assumed" requirements. It's risky to assume that all the requirements specification's readers will know exactly what is intended without the analyst spelling it out. For example, it's not reasonable to think that every reader will automatically know which system functions require the user to be logged in and which do not. It's unrealistic to expect every reader to distinguish those parts of the system that demand particularly rapid response times—and to know just what those response times should be—from the parts that don't have specific performance expectations.

Quality requirements also dictate many architectural choices. If those high-impact requirements aren't written down because the people with that knowledge assume that others share their insight, the product could fail to meet expectations for performance, reliability, integrity, and so forth. An expensive rework project then might begin, building a new architecture to try to meet the demands of the operating environment.

Consider this philosophy: "If it's not in the specification, do not expect to find it in the product." As with all philosophies, this extreme position needs to be tempered by reality. If you attempt to create a totally inclusive specification, you'll spend the rest of your life writing requirements and won't have any time left to build software. My preference, though, is to err in favor of writing down anything you aren't certain that the reader would know. Don't rely on telepathy and clairvoyance as the technical foundations for your project.

Sample Levels of Requirements Detail

Let's return to the home alarm system example from earlier in this chapter. Following is an illustration of how you might write the functional requirements for disarming the triggered system. The first requirement (our original one) is written at a very high level:

Disarm.Alarm: When the alarm system is armed and a sensor is triggered, the user shall be able to enter a numeric passcode to disarm the system.

A developer who receives this requirement likely will have many questions. The following requirements show how the analyst could partially flesh out this high-level requirement with additional specific functional requirements:

Disarm.Alarm	Disarming triggered system with a passcode.
.Sound:	When a sensor is triggered after the system is armed, the alarm system shall emit an intermittent warning tone. The alarm system shall sound the tone until either the system is disarmed or the preset warning duration has passed.
.Interval:	The system shall evaluate an entered passcode 1.0 second following user entry of the last digit. Digits entered within less than 1.0 second of the previous digit's entry are appended to the passcode digits entered so far.
.OK:	If the entered passcode is correct, the system shall stop emitting the warning tone and shall set itself to the disarmed state.
.NoGood:	If the entered passcode is incorrect, the system shall continue to emit the warning tone, continue counting down the warning duration, and permit the user to reenter the passcode.
.Timeout:	If the warning duration is reached before the user enters a valid passcode, the system shall take the following actions:
.Siren:	Trigger the alarm system's siren.
.Dial:	Dial the alarm system monitoring company.
.Log:	Record the alarm incident in the internal system event log.
Warning duration[1] =	* Number of seconds between the time an armed system detects a sensor trigger and the time when the alarm will sound if the system is not disarmed; user programmable; default = 30 seconds.*
Passcode =	* User-entered code to disarm the armed alarm system; must contain 4 to 6 digits inclusive; every digit can be 0 through 9 inclusive; system-supplied default = 1234.*

1. I recommend that you collect data definitions like these in a *data dictionary*, a separate document or an appendix to the SRS where the data elements and data structures that pertain to the requirements are grouped together and hierarchically decomposed (Wiegers 2003a).

Even though these functional requirements answer many of the questions posed earlier in this chapter about the alarm system's behavior, important information is still missing. What is the cycle frequency of the "intermittent warning tone" described in requirement Disarm.Alarm.Sound? How loud is it? What pitch? What does it sound like? I've never seen a requirement that didn't have opportunities for improvement. Whether to specify these details in the requirements or leave them to the developer's judgment is the analyst's call.

You might elect to document your functional requirements at a high level and have developers work with customers to fill in the blanks at design and construction time. Alternatively, you might have your analysts work with customers and subject matter experts to come up with the details and record them in the SRS. Regardless of where you put the information, though, this second example gets closer to what the developers and testers ultimately need to know so that they can build and verify the software.

Chapter 14
To Duplicate or Not to Duplicate

It's not unusual to discover that you need to replicate a specific requirement or piece of requirements-related information in multiple places in your project documentation. This poses a problem that has no perfect solution. On the one hand, it's convenient to be able to view and print all the information associated with a specific issue, topic, function, feature, or use case in a single location. This lets you treat that block of information as a self-contained package. A developer who is responsible for implementing that block will have all the necessary information grouped together.

On the other hand, duplicating information is risky. Even if the same requirement or definition logically fits in several locations, creating multiple instances of it generates a maintenance hazard. Someday you—or someone else—might need to modify that replicated item. There is a very good chance that the modifier *won't* make the same change in every location where the information appears. This introduces an inconsistency that somebody will need to detect and resolve in the future. In addition, replicating information increases the volume of your requirements documentation, and big specifications frighten some people.

 I encountered exactly this situation recently. A client sent me a set of use cases to review. Four of those use cases were influenced by the same business rule. The use case template the client was using included a field for business rules, and each of these four use cases stated the business rule in its entirety in that space. Two of the business rule statements were worded in exactly the same way. The other two were also identical, but they differed slightly from the phrasing used in the first pair. This subtle wording difference immediately raised the question: Are these business rules really the same, or are they different in a small but significant way? The business rules looked to have the same meaning to me, but as a reader of the use case specifications, I really needed to find someone who could confirm this interpretation.

As an alternative to duplicating business rules or other bits of requirements knowledge, consider incorporating cross-references to the original source of the information rather than actually replicating the text wherever it logically belongs. Let me describe several ways to do this.

Cross-Referencing

If you're storing the information in word-processing documents, such as Microsoft Word files, exploit the bookmark and cross-reference functions. In Word, first define a bookmark for the master instance of the replicated information, and give it a unique name. Then, any place you want the same information to reappear, use the Insert Cross-Reference function to insert the bookmarked text wherever you like. The document will look as though exactly the same information is present in multiple places, but the cross-referenced appearances are merely echoes. If you modify the master instance of the bookmarked text and then refresh the display or print the document, the change will immediately be reflected everywhere those cross-references appear.

This approach provides the advantage of having the cross-referenced text appear in all the relevant locations. This gives the reader everything he needs in a single package. It permits unlimited reuse of discrete chunks of information of any size, too. For example, suppose you have a block of five requirements that appear in the description of multiple use cases. You can insert cross-references to visually echo that block of requirements wherever appropriate.

Using cross-references in this fashion does require that the author or maintainer knows where the master copy of the information resides so that he can modify only that occurrence when a change is necessary. Cross-references don't reduce the size of the requirements documentation because the full text of the reused information appears in every pertinent location. Further, cross-references work only within a single document file, not across multiple files. Of course, modifying the master instance—the bookmarked text—won't update any hard copies that already contain an echo of the old version.

Hyperlinks

An alternative strategy is to employ hyperlinks in word-processed, PDF (Adobe Portable Document Format), HTML, or other types of files. In this scheme, you store every unique piece of information in a logically sensible location, typically grouped with other information of the same type. You might collect all business rules in a business rules catalog, all data definitions in a data dictionary, and definitions of key terms in a glossary. Then, any time you need to refer to one of these items in either the same document or another document, you insert a hyperlink to the original place where the information resides.

In the use case example I described earlier, the requirements analyst could have entered just the identifying label and name of the common business rule in the business rules field for all four use cases. It isn't necessary—or desirable—to replicate the full statement of the rule itself in each place. The analyst could make each occurrence of the business rule name or label into a hyperlink to the appropriate entry in the business rules catalog. This gives the reader easy access to that information. Any time the rule changes, only the information at the destination end of the hyperlinks needs to be modified. The hyperlinks will always point to the current and correct instance of that rule. In database terms, this strategy is equivalent to normalizing the database to remove repeated information.

Using hyperlinks in this fashion enhances the maintainability of the requirements data and increases information accuracy. It also reduces the volume of requirements information because each unique piece of information is stored only once. Collecting information of the same type together in one location, as in a business rules catalog, makes it easier to review the information in context. This helps the reviewers to see relationships between the items and to spot duplicates (or worse, near-duplicates), conflicts, errors, and gaps. It also facilitates reuse of common definitions, rules, or requirements across multiple documents and projects within the enterprise.

The big downside to this scheme is that the reader has to follow the links to assemble a full picture of the use case or other package of requirements information. This can be tedious if, say, a use case points to multiple business rules or other external pieces of data. Hyperlinks work well for online navigation, but they aren't so convenient if you want to print out a self-contained portion of the requirements documentation.

Another potential risk with hyperlinks is that changing the master information might require that additional modifications be made in the locations that contain links to that master information. Suppose a data definition is modified in a data dictionary. If the piece of data is reused across projects, there might be three requirements specifications for different projects that all contain hyperlinks to that same data definition. It's possible that other requirements in those three specifications need to be modified to remain consistent with the updated data definition. Without knowing exactly where all these hyperlink instances reside, it's easy to overlook a necessary change in one of those source documents.

Traceability Links

A third option is to store your requirements information in a database, such as that associated with a commercial requirements management tool. You can find descriptions and product feature comparisons for many of the currently available tools at *http://www.paper-review.com/tools/rms/read.php* and *http://www.volere.co.uk/tools.htm*. Requirements management tools allow you to create and populate various requirement classes or types. You can define distinct sets of attributes or metadata for each requirement type. Every object stored in the database receives a unique identifier. You can establish logical connections, called *traceability links* or *traces*, between two objects of the same type or of different types. Requirements management tools overcome some of the limitations of storing requirements in traditional word-processing documents.

Again returning to our use case example, you might create one requirement type of "use case" and another of "business rule" in the requirements management tool. Next, you would store all the pertinent use case descriptions and business rule statements in the database. Then you would create a traceability link between each use case and each business rule that affects that use case, as illustrated in Figure 14-1. This traceability approach facilitates reusing requirement objects not only within a single project, but even across multiple projects. The tool user can traverse the traceability links to access all the information that is logically connected to some entity, such as a specific use case.

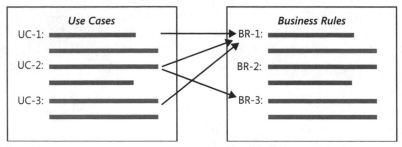

Figure 14-1   Traceability links connect use cases and business rules.

Because each discrete piece of requirement information is stored in a single location, only that one instance must be modified when a change is necessary. The more capable requirements management tools will provide a visual indicator whenever an object on either end of a traceability link changes. This alerts the user to check the object on the other end of the link to see if an update is needed there. For example, if a business rule named BR-3 is changed, any use case that links to BR-3 might also have to be modified. You might also need to update any functional requirements or test cases that trace back to that same use case to keep them consistent with the altered business rule. This multilink tracing is virtually impossible to do by hand; you really need a tool.

Unfortunately, storing the requirements information in a database still makes it hard to pull together all the items that belong to a logical package of requirements information. The ideal requirements management tool would follow the traceability links and insert the information from the destination end of each link into reports generated from the database contents.

Recommendation

There is no perfect solution to the problem of dealing with requirements information that logically fits in more than one place. On balance, I believe the inconvenience of following hyperlinks or traceability links to access connected information beats the maintenance and communication problems caused by duplicating information. Therefore, I recommend that you store each piece of unique requirements information just once. Use one of the mechanisms described in this chapter to point to that master source whenever you need to.

That said, as with all the recommendations in this book, you need to look at each specific situation and do what makes the most sense for that context. There may be times in which it is more convenient or clearer to actually include redundant information. This is analogous to selectively denormalizing a relational database for some legitimate reason. However, you do need to recognize the risk of having one instance of that information fall out of sync with its fellows.

Chapter 15
Elements of Requirements Style

Writing requirements is hard! Actually, writing anything is hard, and writing precise and unambiguous requirements is especially challenging. There is no simple formulaic approach to software specification. High-quality requirements begin with proper grammar, accurate spelling, well-constructed sentences, and a logical organization. This chapter presents several style guidelines to keep in mind when writing functional requirements. Chapter 10 of *Software Requirements, Second Edition* presents additional guidelines for writing clear requirements. It also identifies several dozen ambiguous words and phrases that are best avoided when writing a requirements specification, along with suggestions for more precise alternatives. Hooks and Farry (2001) and Alexander and Stevens (2002) provide many other helpful recommendations for writing better requirements.

I'm not a fan of arbitrary rules about writing requirements. Some I've heard are:

- A requirement may not contain the word *and*. An "and" indicates the presence of two requirements, which must be separated.

- A requirement may not contain more than one sentence.

- A requirement may not contain more than 22 (or was it 23? I can't remember precisely) words.

These sorts of simplistic rules are intended to help analysts write good requirements, but there are too many cases in which they don't constitute good advice. The exceptions don't prove the rule in this case. As you develop your requirements specifications, remember your key objective: clear and effective communication among the project stakeholders.

I Shall Call This a Requirement

Shall is the traditional keyword for identifying a functional requirement. Functional requirements describe behaviors the system shall exhibit under certain circumstances or actions the system shall let the user take.

Some people object to the use of *shall* because it feels stilted.[1] It's not the way people normally talk, at least not outside English period-piece movies. True—but so what? In fact, this is a plus. Using a distinctive word sharply separates a requirement from other information in a specification document. *Shall* serves as a symbol that signals the presence of a discrete requirement.

Too many requirements specifications use a random mix of different verbs: *shall, must, should, could, would, is recommended, is desirable, is requested, will, can, may,* and *might.* Many of these words are used interchangeably in casual conversation. The listener relies on context and the chance to ask for clarification to understand the speaker's point. But this can become confusing in a written specification. The reader is left to wonder whether there's a subtle but important distinction between these various keywords. Does *must* have some different connotation than *can*? Does *might* (which conveys a sense of possibility in normal dialog) mean the same thing as *may* (which conveys a sense of permission)? I've also heard of conventions in which *shall* identifies a requirement, but *will* indicates a design statement and *must* signifies a constraint.

Some organizations follow a convention I find risky. In this scheme, *shall* indicates a function that is required, *should* means that the function is desired, and *may* indicates that the function being described is optional. This raises two problems. First, two concepts are being combined: the statement of intended functionality and the relative priority of that functionality. The second problem is that the priority information is being communicated using words that have similar meaning in everyday conversation. When you use such keyword conventions, you're expecting all readers to understand the priority implied by these words in the same way.[2]

My preference is to use the keyword *shall* to identify functional requirements whenever possible. You might prefer to use *must* as a synonym for *shall,* but sometimes *must* is used to flag a constraint. Avoid *should,*[3] *may, might,* and similar words that don't make it clear whether the statement is a requirement. A requirement in the form, "The system should do X" can be restated in the form, "When Y happens, the system shall do X." Instead of using the shall-should-may convention to communicate priority, I'd rather see three requirements written as follows:

"The system shall ... [Priority = High]."

"The system shall ... [Priority = Medium]."

"The system shall ... [Priority = Low]."

---

1. Some people don't even like the word *requirement* because you rarely implement all of the so-called requirements specified in an SRS. If some function is of low priority—it isn't truly "required"—is it still considered a requirement? Until the software industry changes its vocabulary, yes.

2. For an example of precise definitions that distinguish some of these terms, see "RFC 2119–Keywords for Use in RFCs to Indicate Requirement Levels," which you can find at *http://www.faqs.org/rfcs/rfc2119.html*.

3. My colleague Brian Lawrence suggests that you replace *should* with *probably won't* and see if that would be all right with the customer. It probably won't.

The goal of clear and unambiguous communication is more elusive when requirements writers use a mix of nearly synonymous verbs and expect all readers to reach the same conclusions about what they're trying to say. Frankly, I don't understand the objection to *shall*. It's a clear, strong statement and it's a well-established tradition in requirements engineering. But if you don't like it, pick an alternative word—such as *must*—and use it consistently.

System Perspective or User Perspective?

Various conventions for writing functional requirements exist. Some people believe that requirements should describe only the system's behavior, because "the system" is what you create by implementing all the functional requirements. However, I think it's appropriate to write functional requirements from either the system's perspective or the user's perspective. Use whichever structure offers the clearest communication in a given situation.

Requirements written from the system's perspective conform to the following general structure:

Conditions: "When [some conditions are true] . . ."

Result: ". . . the system shall [do something]"

Qualifier: ". . . [response time goal or quality objective]."

The conditions part of the requirement could reflect an event that triggers the system to respond in some way. Here's a simple example:

> *"When the patron indicates that he does not wish to order any more food items, the system shall display all food items ordered, the individual food item prices, and the total payment amount within 1 second."*

This requirement describes an event that the system can detect, followed by the action the system takes in response to that event. This requirement also includes a performance goal, the 1-second response time. This element constitutes a nonfunctional requirement associated with this specific bit of system functionality.

When stating such performance goals, it's important to make clear whether they are critical values or merely desirable targets. Is the system acceptable if it takes 1.2 seconds to display the order details? How about 10 seconds? Precise response times are more critical for hard real-time systems than for information systems. *Planguage* (plan + language) is an excellent technique for precisely specifying such nonfunctional requirements (Gilb 2005). Planguage contains keywords to distinguish minimally acceptable goals from nominal target values and ideal-case goals.

In some cases, it makes more sense to describe actions that the system will let the user take under particular circumstances. When writing functional requirements from the user's perspective, keep the following general structure in mind (Alexander and Stevens 2002):

User type: "The [user class or actor name] . . ."

Result type: ". . . shall be able to [do something] . . ."

Object: ". . . [to something]."

Qualifier: [response time goal or quality objective]

Alternative phrasings that work well are, "The system shall let (or allow, permit, or enable) the user to [do something]," or "The system shall provide the ability for the user to [do something]." It's more meaningful to refer to the affected user class by name, rather just saying *user*. Here's an illustration of a functional requirement written from the user's perspective:

> *"The patron shall be able to reorder any meal he had ordered within the previous six months, provided that all food items in that order are available on the menu for the meal date."*

Note that these examples are written in the active voice. They explicitly identify the entity—the system or a specific user type—that takes each action. Most of the functional requirements I read are written in passive voice:

> Passive: *"When the output state changes, it is logged in the event log."*

Whenever you can, recast such requirements in the much clearer active voice:

> Active: *"When the output state changes, the system shall record the new state and the time of the state change in the event log."*

With active voice, the reader doesn't have to deduce which entity is doing what. The more explicit and precise you can make the requirements, the easier it will be for the readers to understand them and use them to guide the project work they do.

Parent and Child Requirements

When writing requirements in a hierarchical fashion, the analyst records a parent requirement and one or more child requirements. The parent requirement is satisfied by implementing its children. Here's an illustration of a hierarchical requirement with some problems:

> *3.4 The requester shall enter a charge number for each chemical ordered.*
>
> > *3.4.1 The system shall validate charge numbers against the master corporate charge number list. If the charge number is invalid, the system shall notify the requester and shall not accept the order.*
> >
> > *3.4.2 The charge number entered shall apply to an entire order, not to individual line items in the order.*

Notice that this parent requirement, 3.4, is written in the form of a functional requirement. It's not entirely clear how many requirements are represented here: two or three? Also notice that there is a conflict between the parent requirement and one of its child requirements, 3.4.2. If each ordered chemical is a line item, how many charge numbers is the requester supposed to enter?

These sorts of problems disappear if the parent requirement is written in the form of a heading or title instead of in the form of a functional requirement. Consider using this style whenever you have a set of child requirements that, in the aggregate, constitute a parent requirement. Following is an improved version of the preceding example:

> *3.4 Charge Numbers*
>
> > *3.4.1 The requester shall enter a charge number for each chemical in an order.*
> >
> > *3.4.2 The system shall validate charge numbers against the master corporate charge number list. If the charge number is not found on this list, the system shall notify the requester and shall not accept the order.*

What Was That Again?

Ambiguity is the great bugaboo of software requirements. Ambiguity shows up in two forms. The first form I can catch myself. I read a requirement and realize that I can interpret it in more than one way. I can't determine which interpretation is correct, but at least I caught the ambiguity. There's a joke about the manager of a nuclear power plant who says that the secret of running the plant safely is, "You can't have too much heavy water." Does this mean that if you have too much heavy water you're in trouble, or that the more heavy water you have the better off you are? It could go either way.

The other type of ambiguity is much harder to spot. Suppose the analyst gives the requirements specification to several reviewers. The reviewers encounter an ambiguous requirement that makes sense to each of them but means something different to each of them. The reviewers all report back, "These requirements are fine." They didn't find the ambiguity because each reviewer knows only his own interpretation of that requirement. As a result, there's a good chance that those reviewers will have different expectations and will take different actions because of their diverse understandings of that ambiguous requirement.

The following sections offer some cautions about various sources of ambiguity to watch for and some suggestions about how to write less ambiguous requirements. Nearly all the examples here are drawn from actual SRS documents I have examined.

Complex Logic

Complex Boolean logic offers many opportunities for ambiguities and missing requirements. Consider the following paragraph:

> *If an order is placed for a chemical to a vendor, the system shall check to see if there are any other pending orders for that chemical. If there are, the system shall display the vendor name, vendor catalog number, and the name of the person who placed each previous order. If the user wishes to contact any person who placed a previous order, the system shall allow the user to send that person an e-mail message.*

This long requirement is difficult to read and contains multiple functionality descriptions that should be split into separate requirements. Plus, it has some gaps. Writing requirements in this style makes it difficult to see whether the outcomes of all the if/then branches are specified. "Else" conditions are often overlooked with this sort of textual representation. Nested "or," "and," and "not" clauses are better represented using a decision table or decision tree (Wiegers 2003a). A decision tree such as that shown in Figure 15-1 would immediately reveal that the system's behavior is not specified if there are no pending orders for that particular chemical. Other false outcomes from the decisions are also unspecified. Implicitly, perhaps the reader will conclude that the system should do nothing if the various "if" conditions described here are false, but that's an assumption forced by the incompleteness.

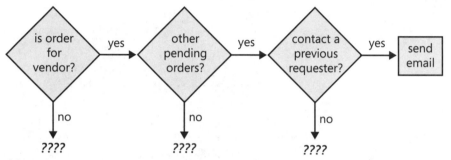

Figure 15-1   Sample decision tree for complex logic.

Expressions involving compound operators—such as "IF this AND (that OR the other)"—are even more confusing:

> *If the amount of the cash refund is less than $50 or the amount of the cash refund is $50 or greater and the current user is a supervisor, then the system shall open the cash register drawer.*

Making this requirement understandable and unambiguous requires either parentheses (awkward) or splitting into multiple requirements (better).

Negative Requirements

Negative (or inverse) requirements are another source of confusion. When I read a requirement that describes a behavior the system is *not* supposed to exhibit, I realize that I've already satisfied the requirement and I don't even work on the project! Anybody can make the system do nothing. Try to recast inverse requirements in a positive sense, to state what the system *will* do under certain circumstances. Constraining business rules sometimes describe actions that specific users are not permitted to take. This isn't a desirable characteristic of functional requirements, though.

Table 15-1 states several real functional requirements that contain negation, along with possible ways to rewrite them in a positive sense. I've also restated these passive-voice requirements into the less ambiguous active voice, which clearly shows what entity is taking each action.

Note that changing a negative requirement into a positive one often requires inserting the word *only* to identify the conditions that permit the system action being described to take place.

Table 15-1   Removing Negation from Functional Requirements

Before	After
All users with three or more accounts should not be migrated.	The system shall migrate only users having fewer than three accounts.
The registration process will default to International English and will not present a localized experience until country and language are selected.	The registration process shall default to International English. After the user selects the country and language, the registration process shall present a localized experience.
A domain name cannot be transferred to another registrar during the registration grace period.[1]	The domain administrator may transfer a domain name to another registrar only after the registration grace period.
The PC administrator will not have the ability to change the FZL-Web user.	Only the system administrator shall be able to change the FZL-Web user.

1. Note also the ambiguity between *cannot* (as in "not able to") and *may not* (as in "not permitted to").

Avoid double and triple negatives in all circumstances. Consider this example:

> *Training rewards and points will not be visible to users who cannot participate in training rewards.*

We can rephrase this double negative into a positive statement that's easier to understand:

> *The system shall display training rewards and points only to users who are permitted to participate in training rewards.*

Following is another illustration of recasting a double negative into a positive using an "only" constraint. The original requirement said:

> *Users who are delivered service without being authenticated should not generate accounting records.*

Let's state it as a positive action that the developer can actually implement:

> *The system shall generate accounting records only for users who are delivered service after being authenticated.*

Multiple negations can lead to ambiguous requirements, as illustrated here:

> *Records, however, should not fail validation if these attributes are not present at all.*

Does this mean that the records *should* fail validation if the attributes are present? Probably not. The context might make the meaning of this requirement clearer, but as it's written, it raises a question in my mind. The main message here is to think positive when writing requirements!

Omissions

Requirements sometimes lack important bits of information. This makes it hard for all readers to interpret them in the same way unless they make precisely the same assumptions. A requirement might describe a behavior without identifying the triggering cause that leads to that behavior:

> *The system shall generate an error report and forward it to the user.*

This requirement doesn't identify the stimulus that leads the system to produce the error report. Another common type of error involves missing descriptions of how possible exceptions should be handled. In the previous example, what should happen if no errors occur during the processing being described? It's unspecified, thereby leaving it up to the developer to decide what to do. Options include:

- Do nothing (an assumed default perhaps).
- Present a "Congratulations! No errors found." message but do not generate a report.
- Generate an empty report and forward it to the user.
- Generate a report stating that no errors were found and forward it to the user.

Perhaps we add the following requirement to address the case in which no errors are encountered:

> *If parsing is successful, the system shall not generate an error report.*

This is another description of the system doing nothing, though, as we discussed under "Negative Requirements" earlier in this section. It would be better to state what the system *will* do if no error is encountered, even if it is to simply continue the processing.

Another kind of incompleteness occurs when requirements describe system behaviors that involve some type of symmetry. Suppose you're specifying the functional requirements for a bookmark feature in a Web browser. You might say:

> *The system shall display the user's defined bookmarks in a collapsible hierarchical tree structure.*

So, the user can collapse the bookmark tree, but what if he wants to expand it again? It's easy to overlook that sort of symmetrical or reverse operation. To remedy this, either you could add a second requirement stating that the tree can be expanded, or you could alter this requirement to say ". . . in a collapsible and expandable hierarchical tree structure."

If you leave out the reverse operation, the customer and the analyst might assume that the missing portion of the symmetrical requirement is implied. If you request an undo capability, of course you want a redo capability as well, right? But implicit requirements make me nervous. They involve too many assumptions about the knowledge and thought processes that other stakeholders must have to ensure that we all get what we expect in the final product. I know of an organization that developed its own tool for editing and storing source code in a database, with no written requirements. Unfortunately, they forgot to include the ability to print the contents of the database. The team members no doubt assumed that a printing function would be included, so they didn't even think to mention it. They didn't mention it, and they didn't get it.

Boundaries

Boundary values in numerical ranges provide additional opportunities for creating ambiguity, as well as being places to look for missing requirements. Suppose you're writing software for a point-of-sale system and you need to comply with a business rule that states, "Only supervisors may issue cash refunds greater than $50." An analyst might derive several functional requirements from that business rule, such as the following:

1. *If the amount of the cash refund is less than $50, the system shall open the cash register drawer.*

2. *If the amount of the cash refund is more than $50 and the user is a supervisor, the system shall open the cash register drawer. If the user is not a supervisor, the system shall display a message: "Call a supervisor for this transaction."*

But what if the amount of the cash refund is exactly $50? Is this a third, unspecified case? Or is it one of the two cases already described? If so, which one? Such ambiguity forces the developer either to make his best guess or to track down the person who can answer the question definitively. This is an example of the analyst generating an inconsistency between a higher-level piece of information—the business rule—and the functional requirements derived from it.

You can resolve boundary ambiguities in one of two ways. The previous requirement #1 could be rewritten as, "If the amount of the cash refund is less than *or equal to* $50, the system shall open the cash register drawer." This preserves the original intent of the business rule and eliminates the ambiguity.

Alternatively, you could use the words *inclusive* and *exclusive* to explicitly indicate whether the endpoints of a numerical range are considered to lie within the range or outside the range. To illustrate with a different example, you might say, "The system shall calculate a 20% discount on orders of 6 to 10 units, inclusive." This wording makes it perfectly clear that both endpoints of the range, 6 and 10, lie within the range subject to the 20-percent price discount. You still need to review a set of similar requirements to make sure the range endpoints don't overlap, though. For example, note the inconsistency between the following two requirements:

1. *The system shall calculate a 20% discount on orders of 6 to 10 units, inclusive.*

2. *The system shall calculate a 30% discount on orders of 10 to 20 units, inclusive.*

The boundary value of 10 is incorrectly included in both ranges. Using a table to show this sort of information is more concise and makes these kinds of errors more evident:

Units Purchased	Discount Percentage
1–5	0
6–10	20
11–20	30
21+	40

Avoiding Ambiguous Wording

The following sections offer some guidelines for writing requirements more precisely to avoid some of the pitfalls of ambiguous language.

Synonyms   I once reviewed some requirements for software that controlled several analytical chemistry instruments in a laboratory. In some places, the analyst who wrote the specification referred to "chemical samples," and in other places she referred to "runs." I asked her about the difference between a sample and a run. "They're really the same thing," she replied. I suggested she pick one term and stick to her story. Whenever I read a document that uses slightly different terms to refer to the same item, I have to check with someone to ascertain whether they are truly synonyms. Place such definitions in a shared glossary so that team members can use them consistently throughout the project and perhaps even across multiple projects.

Near-synonyms   Elsewhere in that same SRS the author had used three terms that I thought might be synonyms. When I inquired, I learned that they had subtly different meanings. Define such terms in your project glossary to ensure that all readers can reach the same understanding of the terms.

Pronouns   My mother is a known pronoun abuser. She will say something like, "He said he'd bring that down as soon as he was done with it," and I'll have no idea who or what she is talking about. Pronouns also can be a source of confusion in a requirements specification. Be certain that the antecedent is crystal clear whenever you employ a pronoun. If you use a word such as *this* or *that*, there should be no confusion in the reader's mind about what you're referring to.

The abbreviations *i.e.* and *e.g.*   Another ambiguity risk involves using abbreviations that some readers might misconstrue. A common point of confusion is the use of *i.e.* versus *e.g.* Consider the following requirement from an actual specification:

> *The program needs to have a means of allowing the operator to manually activate certain portions of the process in the event a mistake is made (i.e., activate the valve set to apply pressure or vacuum, set pressures, and activate the temperature chamber).*

The abbreviation *i.e.* stands for the Latin phrase *id est*, which means "that is." The abbreviation *e.g.* stands for the Latin phrase *exempli gratia*, which means "for example." These two abbreviations are so commonly confused that I don't trust their use in a requirements specification unless I'm positive that the author understands the difference. In the previous example, the use of *i.e.* indicates that the following list itemizes *all* portions of the process that require a means of manual activation. However, if the author really meant for these to be just examples— a portion of that set—he should have used *e.g.* instead. That way, the reader knows that many more such manual activations could be needed. Unfortunately, the reader won't have any idea how many more activations might be needed or just what those activations are from this requirement. It's essential to make it clear whether you are presenting a complete list of items or just an illustrative subset. I suggest explicitly saying *for example* instead of *e.g.* so that every reader knows what you mean.

A/B   Some specification writers use an A/B writing construct, as in the following example:

> *Prior to operator intervention, a snapshot of this data should be recorded in an audit/ history table.*

What exactly does this mean? Is this requirement referring to an audit table, a history table, a history of audits, or an audit of histories? Are both kinds of information stored in the same table, or are audits the same as histories, or what? Other than *and/or*, *read/write*, and a few others, the A/B construct is rarely used in formal writing because it is so ambiguous. When I see that construct, I can think of five possible interpretations, but I don't know which one is correct in the given situation:

- A is the same as B. (If A and B are synonyms, use just one term consistently.)

- Both A and B. (Use the explicit conjunction *and*.)

- A or B. (Use the explicit conjunction *or*.)

- A is the opposite of B, as in "approving/disapproving changes." (Use the conjunctions *and* and *or* as appropriate to convey the correct meaning.)

- "I'm not sure just what I'm thinking here, so I'll leave it up to each reader to decide what he thinks this means." (Decide exactly what you intend to say, and choose the right words.)

Similar-sounding words   Writers sometimes write one word but mean another. As an illustration, I often hear people say, "I'll flush out that specification some more," when they really mean, "I'll flesh out that specification some more." Hunters *flush* their prey from their hiding places, but analysts *flesh* out their requirements to give them more substance. Consider the following example, drawn from an actual SRS for a telephony product:

> *Phone Company caller tunes (default) will take priority over all configured individual caller settings that a customer has selected. However, if an individual has been assigned a Phone Company caller tune for the same date, this will overwrite the Phone Company caller tune.*

You *overwrite* a piece of data, but you *override* a default value. In this context, either interpretation is potentially correct, so it's imperative that the author chooses the right word. Watch out for these common types of errors, which sometimes arise from mispronunciations in speech. Keep a dictionary handy so that you can be sure which word to use. A useful reference for common word usage errors in English is provided by Paul Brians at *http://www.wsu.edu/~brians/errors/errors.html* (2003).

Adverbs   Words that end in *-ly* often are ambiguous. They might describe some desirable property of the product, but exactly what is desired is left to each reader's interpretation. Here are some real examples of ineffective adverb usage in requirements specifications:

- Provide a *reasonably* predictable end-user experience.

- Offer *significantly* better download times.

- Optimize upload and download to perform *quickly*.

- Performance for these users should *broadly* match those for . . .

- Downloading this file should complete in *approximately* 15 minutes.

- Exposing information *appropriately* . . .

- Allows the user to edit his interests and *possibly* search results . . .

- Request formats sent by customers must be *clearly* defined.

- Subscribers who are changing content selection (*effectively* a subset of the currently subscribed subscribers) . . .

- *Generally* incurs a "per unit" cost . . .

- To enable remedial action to be initiated in a *timely* manner . . .

- . . . as *expediently* as possible . . .

- *Occasionally* (not very *frequently*) there will be an error condition . . .

Some other adverbs to use with caution are *directly, easily, frequently, ideally, instantaneously, normally, optionally, periodically, preferably, rapidly, transparently, typically,* and *usually*. Try to be more specific when describing the intended product characteristics so that all readers will share a common vision of what result they will have when they're done.

You won't learn how to write good requirements from reading a book on software requirements engineering or a book on technical writing. You need practice. Write requirements to the best of your ability, and then enlist some of your colleagues to review them. Constructive feedback from reviewers can help anyone become a better writer. In fact, it's essential. Requirements quality is in the eye of the reader of the requirements, not the author. No matter how fine the author thinks the requirements are, the ultimate arbiters are those who must base their own work on those requirements.

Chapter 16

The Fuzzy Line Between Requirements and Design

It's often said that requirements are about what you build and design is about how you build it. But there are two problems with this simplistic demarcation.

First, this statement makes it sound as though there's a sharp boundary between requirements and design. There's not. In reality, the distinction between requirements and design is a fuzzy gray region, not a crisp black line. I prefer to say that requirements should emphasize *what* and design should emphasize *how*. It is often valuable to take some tentative steps into the solution space and explore possible designs that might satisfy some requirements you have in hand. This exploration is a way to assess the clarity, correctness, completeness, and feasibility of those requirements. Prototyping is a valuable technique for making some preliminary probes into design (Wiegers 2003a). Getting customer feedback on user interface prototypes or assessing the viability of technical prototypes is an excellent way to confirm that your requirements explorations are on the right track.

A second problem is that one observer's *how* is another person's *what* (Davis 1993). It's really a matter of abstraction. Figure 16-1 illustrates an abstraction scale for the sequence of moving from some motivation for executing a software project down to the nuts and bolts of exactly how the software is implemented. You can think of each pair of adjacent steps in this scale as representing a kind of *what* information at the higher abstraction level and a kind of *how* information at the lower abstraction level.

Look at the second box from the top in Figure 16-1. If we asked, "What will the user be able to do with this product?" we might come up with several use cases, scenarios, or stories that describe user interactions with the product that lead to some useful outcomes. If we then asked, "How will we let the user perform those use cases?" we might come up with a list of specific features, functional requirements, and product characteristics, shown in the next box down. This information answers the question, "What should the developer build?" The sequence of what and how relationships continues to the lowest level of abstraction.

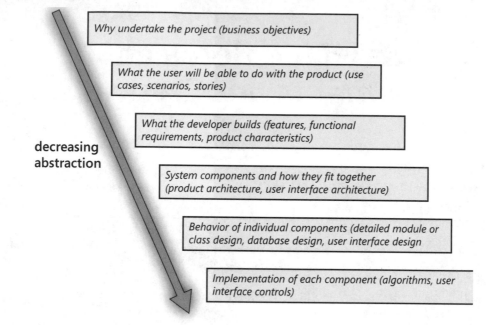

Figure 16-1   Levels of abstraction in software specification and development.

Solution Ideas and Design Constraints

When it comes to requirements specification and design, the essential issue is not one of *what* versus *how*. It's a question of distinguishing the real customer need from just one possible description of how a clever developer might satisfy that need. Incorporating a solution idea into a requirement imposes a design constraint. The requested solution describes one way to satisfy some requirement but perhaps not the only way, the best way, or even a good way. Focusing on solutions masks the underlying requirement. This can make it difficult for a developer to understand what the customer is really trying to do, making it hard to devise the most appropriate approach to meet that expectation.

Legitimate design constraints are perfectly appropriate. In fact, it's critical for developers to know about them. Including the rationale behind imposed constraints along with the requirement can preempt questions that might otherwise arise as developers wonder if they have any design latitude. The risk is that requirements discussions will focus on solutions that the customer or analyst thought of and will impose unnecessary constraints. This is frustrating for developers and often leads to a suboptimal outcome. One of my consulting clients described her experience with this sort of situation:

> *One of the biggest issues I am having with the client support staff is that they focus on the solution. They work closely with the customer and, instead of understanding the business problem or need of the customer, they focus immediately on a solution. We just wasted*

30 hours of the company's time in meetings over one custom project because the client support person proposed a solution and didn't share pertinent user requirements with the business analyst. This is very inefficient and frustrating for meeting participants.

I'm more comfortable with requirements that contain design constraints when the requirements are specifying enhancements to be made to an existing system, rather than for new product development. A current product necessarily imposes many constraints.[1] Designers must respect the architecture and external interface conventions that are built into the current product. You certainly don't want designers coming up with user interface displays that differ radically from those to which the users are already accustomed, as that would compromise usability. The requirements for an enhancement or modification might deal simply with changing a screen layout, adding a new input field or two, modifying the database to accommodate the new data elements, revising a report, and the like. Such changes must integrate smoothly with the existing reality, so constraints are natural in these situations.

Rather than getting hung up on whether the specifications for these modifications constitute requirements or design, remember the key objective of requirements development: clear and effective communication. The analyst should document whatever information is necessary to make sure that the correct changes are implemented in the current product. Beware of a premature emphasis on the solution that doesn't carefully consider the problem to be solved and that doesn't ensure that the specified solution is a good option.

Solution Clues

The requirements analyst needs to detect when a requirement imposes unnecessary constraints on designers. This should lead to a discussion with the customer representatives about the underlying need that led to the customer proposing that specific solution. It's important to respect the customer's input. Don't summarily dismiss the customer's solution idea; important information is hiding in there somewhere. Use that input as a starting point to drill down to a deeper understanding of what the customer is really trying to accomplish. It's possible that the customer's solution idea will be appropriate, but don't let the customer—or any other stakeholder—paint the development team into a constraint corner prematurely.

Asking "why" several times is often a good way to arrive at this understanding. (See Chapter 7, "An Inquiry, Not an Inquisition.") The analyst must determine which of the following situations applies when he hears a proposed solution:

- Did the solution just pop into the speaker's mind as a possible option to consider?
- Is this the only possible solution (that is, a true constraint)?

---

1. Of course, new development projects are also subject to constraints, such as when the new product is a member of an existing product family, is being built from a common product platform, or must integrate into a specific operating environment.

- Is the speaker more interested in exploring solutions (which is fun) than in understanding the problem (which is hard)?

- Is this a poor solution because the problem isn't properly defined or the solution addresses the wrong problem?

- Does someone think this is a fitting solution for some inappropriate reason, such as an erroneous assumption or an unnecessary continuation of the way work was done in the past?

- Is the solution idea worth passing along to developers as a clearly labeled suggestion but not as a mandated requirement?

One clue that the discussion has moved into solution space is that the customer requests that specific technologies or user interface controls be used without a clear justification. If there is indeed a good reason to impose the design constraint, including that explanation in a "rationale" requirement attribute will help the readers. Following are some examples of requirements that contain solutions, several of which are drawn from actual project SRS documents:

- "The Defect Calculator should be written in Microsoft Excel." Whenever an analyst hears a requirement like this, he should ask, "Why?" Why Excel? Perhaps there's an excellent reason, in which case it might be just fine to include the technology constraint in the requirement, along with an explanation of why that constraint was imposed. However, maybe there's nothing magical or essential about using Excel, and the developers should be free to explore other approaches.

- "A master power button shall be installed on the front panel." Further discussion might surface an explanation of why this precise design approach is necessary. Perhaps it's required for compatibility with an existing product, or maybe it will conform to a pertinent standard or safety requirement. Or it could be an unstated ease-of-use requirement. If so, it would be good to know about any related usability requirements that could influence this, and possibly other, functionality or design issues.

- "If the pressure in the tank exceeds 40 PSI, the system shall illuminate the amber pressure warning light." The analyst could ask whether this requirement should be made more abstract to permit the designer to consider various ways to alert the operator about the high tank pressure. But the customer might respond, "No, the operator console has an amber warning light for exactly this purpose, and it had better come on if the pressure exceeds the limit." This would be an example of an appropriate design constraint.

- "The user clicks OK to submit the request." Perhaps it would be clearer for the button to be labeled Submit Request rather than OK. This requirement also assumes that the user will be employing a WIMP (windows, icons, mouse, and pointing device) interface. If the product's user interface has already been implemented and we're adding an enhancement to it, it's fine for the requirement to include the precise user action that will submit the request. However, if you're specifying a new product, avoid constraining the user interface options at an early stage with a requirement such as this. Maybe it would make more sense in the operating environment to use a touch screen display, a command-line interface, or even speech recognition. A more general version of this requirement would simply say, "The user shall be able to submit the request," which leaves to the designer the specifics of how to perform that action.

- "The Background Task Manager shall display error messages in the status bar." If the application already contains a status bar where users are accustomed to seeing messages, this is the right requirement. But what if the decision hasn't yet been made to include a status bar in the user interface? This requirement imposes a design constraint by demanding that a status bar be used for displaying messages. That constraint precludes a creative developer from conceiving other, perhaps better, ways to present error messages.

Taking the time to drill down to the underlying requirement behind a presented solution can pay off. In the early 1980s, my small software group was implementing a PC-based program to control some equipment in a laboratory. This was long before we had multitasking operating systems. One of our users asked us to write a pop-up calculator program to go along with this control software. The developer's reaction was, "Cool! I'd love to write a pop-up calculator program." But then we thought about it some more.

The underlying need was for the user to be able to perform calculations while the computer was busy running the lab equipment. We concluded that it would be much cheaper to buy each of our 150 users a nice handheld calculator, put a piece of Velcro on the back, and mount it on the side of the computer monitor. This solution wasn't nearly as entertaining as writing a pop-up calculator program, but it was a lot less expensive. With either approach, the customer's need was met. And that's the bottom line in software development.

Part VI
On the Requirements Process

Everybody talks about project scope, but it's not easy to find information about good ways to represent scope. Chapter 17, "Defining Project Scope," presents three techniques for distinguishing the contents of your next product release from excluded functionality and external entities that must interface with your product. Chapter 18, "The Line in the Sand," deals with another difficult question: knowing when it's appropriate to baseline a set of requirements. Numerous factors are presented to contemplate before your team defines a requirements baseline.

Although the analyst's natural inclination is to document requirements in the form of structured natural language text, representing requirements using a variety of techniques adds considerable value. If you create multiple requirements views at various levels of abstraction, the specification readers will gain a richer understanding of the intended product. As Chapter 19, "The Six Blind Men and the Requirements," points out, these different views also provide a powerful technique for discovering requirements errors and omissions.

Chapter 17
Defining Project Scope

Every software team talks about project scope, and team members often complain about unending scope creep. Unfortunately, the software industry lacks uniform definitions of these terms. Even worse, the requirements engineering literature is short on clear guidance regarding how to represent scope. In this chapter, I present some definitions, describe three techniques for defining project scope (the context diagram, the use case diagram, and feature levels), and offer some tips for managing scope creep.

Vision and Scope

The vision and scope document is a key software project deliverable (Wiegers 2003a). You can find a suggested template for this document at *http://www.processimpact.com/goodies .shtml*. Other terms for this type of guiding document are a *project charter*, *marketing requirements document*, and *business case*. Any project of any size will benefit from such strategic guidance, even if it consists of only a paragraph at the beginning of an SRS instead of a comprehensive, standalone document.

Vision and scope are two related concepts. I think in terms of the *product vision* and the *project scope*. Both the vision and the scope are components of the project's business requirements. I define the product vision like this:

> *A long-term strategic concept of the ultimate purpose and form of a new system.*

The product vision could also describe the product's place among its competition and in its market or operating environment. Chapter 5 of *Software Requirements, Second Edition* describes how to write a concise and focused vision statement using a simple keyword template.

We can define the project scope as the following:

> *The portion of the ultimate product vision that the current project will address. The scope draws the boundary between what's in and what's out for the project.*

The latter part of the project scope definition is most important. The scope identifies what the product is and is not, what it will and won't do, what it will and won't contain. A well-defined scope sets expectations among the project stakeholders. It defines the external interfaces between the rest of the world and the system, which could be just a software application or could combine automation elements with manual processes. The scope definition helps the project manager assess the resources needed to implement the project and to make realistic commitments. In essence, the scope statement defines the boundary of the project manager's responsibilities.

Your scope definition also should include a list of specific limitations or exclusions—what's out. Obviously, you can't list *everything* that's out of scope because that would include every detail in the universe except for the tiny sliver that is in scope for your project. Instead, the limitations should identify capabilities that a reader might expect to be included in the project but are not included. One project that I know of—a Web site for a national sports team—included the following scope exclusions for the initial release:

- There will be no virtual or fantasy games via the Web.
- There will be no ticketing facilities on the site.
- There will be no betting facilities available.
- The demographic details for newsletters will not be collected.
- Message boards are out of scope for phase 1.

Some stakeholders involved with this Web site project might have expected these capabilities to be included with the first release. Itemizing them as exclusions makes it clear that they won't be. This is a form of expectation management.

Context Diagram

The *context diagram* is a venerable analysis model that dates from the structured analysis revolution of the 1970s (DeMarco 1979; Wiegers 2003a). Despite its age, the context diagram remains a useful way to depict the environment in which a software system exists. Figure 17-1 illustrates a partial context diagram for a hypothetical corporate cafeteria ordering system. The context diagram shows the name of the system or product of interest in a circle. The circumference of the circle represents the system boundary. Rectangles outside the circle represent *external entities*, also called *terminators*. External entities could be user classes, actors, organizations, other software systems to which this one connects, or hardware devices that interface to the system. The interfaces between the system and these external entities are shown with the labeled arrows, called *flows*. Flows represent the movement of data, control signals, or physical objects between the system and the external entities.[1] Two-headed flows indicate read/write or update operations involving the data object on the flow.

---

1. If a "system" is considered to include both a software application and manual operations, flows could represent the movement of physical objects. However, if the system is strictly an automated system involving software and perhaps hardware components, flows represent data or control signals.

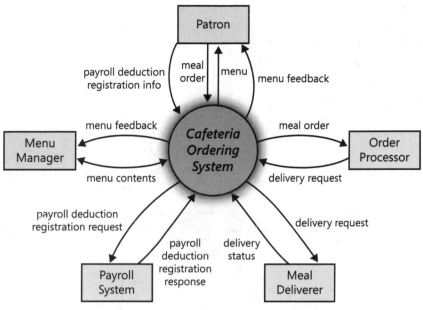

Figure 17-1 A sample context diagram.

The context diagram depicts the project scope at a high level of abstraction. This diagram deliberately reveals nothing about the system internals, including functionality, architecture, and look and feel. Nor does it explicitly identify which features or functionality are in scope and which are not. The functional behavior of the system is merely implied by the labeled flows that connect the system to the external entities. Even the flows are labeled at a high level of abstraction, just to keep the diagram's complexity manageable. Data flows can be decomposed into individual data elements in the project's data dictionary or data model. Corresponding data inputs and outputs suggest the types of transactions or use cases that the system will perform, but these items are not shown explicitly in the context diagram.

Despite the limited view that the high level of abstraction imposes, the context diagram is a helpful representation of scope. An analyst in a requirements seminar I once taught showed me a context diagram for her current project. She had recently shown this diagram to the project manager. The manager had pointed out that one of the external entities on the context diagram—another information system—was now going to be part of the new project. If the diagram was that shown in Figure 17-1, this would be comparable to moving the Payroll System inside the project circle. That is, the scope of the project just got larger. This analyst had expected that external system to be someone else's responsibility, but now it was her problem. The context diagram provides a tool to help the project stakeholders communicate a common understanding of what lies outside the system boundary.

A context diagram could represent either the ultimate vision for the final product or the scope for a specific project that will implement just one of the releases planned for that product. Both uses of context diagrams are appropriate, but be sure to label your diagrams so that readers know exactly what they're viewing.

Use Case Diagram

Use cases have become widely recognized as a powerful technique for exploring user requirements (Kulak and Guiney 2004; Wiegers 2003a). The Unified Modeling Language, or UML, includes a use case diagram notation, which I introduced in Chapter 10, "Actors and Users." Figure 17-2 shows a partial use case diagram for our cafeteria ordering system.

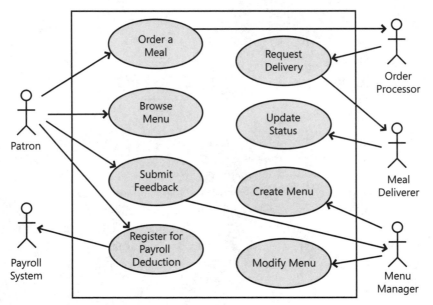

Figure 17-2   A sample use case diagram.

The rectangular box represents the system boundary, analogous to the circle in a context diagram. The stick figures outside the box represent actors, entities that reside outside the system's context but interact with the system in some way. The actors correspond approximately to the external entities shown in rectangles on the context diagram, although the context diagram might include user classes as well as actors.

Unlike the context diagram, the use case diagram does provide limited visibility into the system. Each oval inside the system boundary box represents a use case. The context diagram shows the system's relationship with its environment, including other systems, and the flow of data between them. The use case diagram shows the interactions of the system with its users and some connections between internal system operations, albeit at a high level of abstraction.

The arrows on the use case diagram indicate which actors participate in each use case. (See Chapter 10 for more information about actors and use cases.) Arrows do not indicate data flows as they do on the context diagram. Some analysts simply draw lines instead of arrows on the use case diagram to avoid any confusion with data flow. In addition to showing these connections to external actors, a use case diagram could depict logical relationships and dependencies between use cases.

The use case diagram provides a richer scope representation than the context diagram because it provides a high-level look at the system's capabilities, not just at its external interfaces. There is a practical limitation, though. Any sizeable software system will have dozens of use cases, with many connections between them and between use cases and actors. Attempting to show all those objects inside a single system boundary box quickly becomes unwieldy. Therefore, the analyst needs to model groups of related use cases as packages or to create multiple use case diagrams at various levels of abstraction (Armour and Miller 2001).

Feature Levels

Customers, marketers, and developers often talk about product features, but the software industry doesn't have a standard definition of this term. In Chapter 1, "Fundamentals of Software Requirements," I defined a *feature* as the following:

> *A set of logically related functional requirements that provides a capability to the user and enables the satisfaction of a business objective.*

Features are product capabilities that are recognizable to a user, as opposed to capabilities that the product needs to have but that are not visible to end users. Marketing materials often state the features that the new (or improved) product will offer to the customer. Therefore, features help customers make purchase decisions.

You can think of each product feature as having a series of levels that represent increasing degrees of capability or feature enrichment.[2] Each release of the product implements a certain set of new features and perhaps enhances features that were partially implemented in earlier releases. One way to describe the scope of a particular product release, then, is to identify the specific levels for each feature that the team will implement in that release. A sequence of releases represents increasing levels of capability—and hence user value—delivered over a period of time. During requirements analysis, the analyst determines just which functional requirements must be implemented in a particular release to deliver the planned feature levels, beginning with the top-priority levels of the top-priority features.

To illustrate this approach to scope definition, consider the following set of features from our cafeteria ordering system:

FE-1: Create and modify cafeteria menus.

FE-2: Order meals from the cafeteria menu to be picked up or delivered.

---

2. Nejmeh and Thomas (2002) use the term *feature vector* to refer to a single feature and the various functional levels that a feature implementation can achieve.

FE-3: Order meals from local restaurants to be delivered.

FE-4: Register for meal payment options.

FE-5: Request meal delivery.

FE-6: Establish, modify, and cancel meal service subscriptions.

FE-7: Produce recipes and ingredient lists for custom meals from the cafeteria.

Table 17-1 illustrates a *feature roadmap*, which depicts the various levels for each of these features that are planned for implementation in forthcoming releases. FE-2 and FE-5 in Table 17-1 represent features that each have three enrichment levels. The full functionality for each of these features is delivered incrementally across the three planned releases. The analyst can also indicate dependencies between features or feature levels. As an illustration, the level of FE-2 scheduled for release 1 is expected to let users pay for meals by payroll deduction. Therefore, the capability of FE-4 that lets users register for payroll deduction payments cannot be deferred to a later release because FE-2 depends on FE-4.

Table 17-1   A Sample Feature Roadmap

Feature	Release 1	Release 2	Release 3
FE-1	Fully implemented		
FE-2	Standard individual meals from lunch menu only; delivery orders may be paid for only by payroll deduction (depends on FE-4)	Accept orders for breakfasts and dinners, in addition to lunches; accept credit and debit card payments	Accept group meal orders for meetings and events
FE-3	Not implemented	Not implemented	Fully implemented
FE-4	Register for payroll deduction payments only	Register for credit card and debit card payments	
FE-5	Meals will be delivered only to company campus sites	Add delivery from cafeteria to selected off-site locations	Add delivery from restaurants to all current delivery locations
FE-6	Implemented if time permits	Fully implemented	
FE-7	Not implemented	Not implemented	Fully implemented

The feature level approach is the most descriptive of the three techniques presented in this chapter for defining the project scope. The farther into the future you look, the less certain the scope plans become and the more you can expect to adjust the scope as project and business realities change. Nonetheless, defining the product vision and project scope lays a solid foundation for the rest of the project work. This helps keep the team on track toward maximizing stakeholder satisfaction.

Managing Scope Creep

Requirements will change and grow over the course of any software project. This is a natural aspect of software development. In fact, if a project doesn't experience some level of growth, the team likely is ignoring reality and risks releasing an irrelevant product. Therefore, the project manager needs to anticipate and plan for some requirements growth.

Scope creep (also known as *feature creep*, *requirements creep*, *featuritis*, and *creeping featurism*) refers to the uncontrolled growth of functionality that the team attempts to stuff into an already-full project box. It doesn't all fit. The continuing churn and expansion of the requirements, coupled with a lack of rigorous prioritization, make it difficult to deliver the most important functionality on schedule. This demand for ever-increasing functionality leads to delays, quality problems, and misdirected energy. Scope creep is one of the most pervasive challenges of software development.

The first step in controlling scope creep is to document a clearly stated—and agreed-upon—scope for the project. Without such a scope definition, how can you even tell if you're experiencing scope creep? The techniques described earlier in this chapter provide several ways to define a project's scope. Project teams following an agile development life cycle should write a brief scope statement for every iteration cycle to make sure everyone understands the goal of the iteration and what functionality the team will implement during that iteration.

An ill-defined scope boundary can have serious consequences. In one situation I know of, a customer had hired a package-solution vendor to migrate three sets of existing data into the new package. Partway through the project, the customer concluded that six additional data conversions were required. The customer felt that this additional work lay within the agreed-upon scope, but the vendor maintained that it was out of scope and demanded additional payment. This scope ambiguity was one factor that led to the project being cancelled and a lawsuit being filed (Wiegers 2003b).

The second step for managing scope creep is to ask "Is this in scope?" whenever someone proposes some additional product capability, such as a use case, functional requirement, product feature, or output. Note that the project scope could also encompass activities and deliverables besides the delivered software products themselves. Perhaps your customers request an online tutorial to help their users learn the new system. This doesn't change the software product itself, but it certainly expands the scope of the overall project.

There are three possible answers to the question, "Is this in scope?" If the new capability is clearly in scope, the team needs to address it. If it's clearly out of scope, the team does not need to address it, at least not now. They might schedule the new capability for a later release.

Sometimes, though, the requested functionality lies outside the scope as it's currently defined but is such a good idea that the management sponsor should expand the project scope to accommodate it. Less frequently, a proposed change could even modify the strategic product vision in some fundamental way. The question to consider is whether the proposal to expand the scope of the current release will significantly enhance the success of that release.

Electing to increase project scope is a business decision. When weighing whether to increase project scope, the key stakeholders need to consider cost, risk, schedule, and market or business implications. This demands negotiation between the project manager, the management sponsor, and key customers to determine how best to handle the scope alteration. That is, the owner of the business requirements—the management sponsor—must decide whether proposed changes in user or functional requirements will become the project manager's responsibility through a scope expansion. (See Figure 17-3.) Following are some possible strategies for accommodating a scope increase:

■ Defer or eliminate some lower-priority functionality that was planned for the current release to make room for the proposed additions to the scope.

■ Obtain additional development staff to handle the additional work.

■ Obtain additional funding, perhaps to pay overtime (OK, this is just a little joke), outsource some work, or purchase productivity tools.

■ Extend the schedule for the current release to accommodate the extra functionality. (This is not a joke.)

■ Compromise on quality by doing a hasty job that you'll need to repair later on (not your best option).

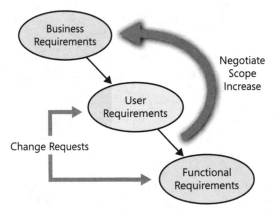

Figure 17-3   Changes in user and functional requirements lead to negotiations about increasing project scope at the business requirements level.

Increasing scope (or, even more profoundly, vision) always has a price. The people who are paying for the project must make a considered decision as to which scope management strategy is most appropriate in each situation. The objective is always to deliver the maximum customer value, while achieving the defined business objectives and success criteria, within the existing constraints.

There's no point in pretending that the project team can implement an ever-increasing quantity of functionality without paying a price. In addition, it's always prudent to anticipate a certain amount of scope growth over the course of the project. The savvy project manager will incorporate contingency buffers into project plans so that the team can accommodate some scope growth without demolishing its schedule commitments (Wiegers 2002b; DeMarco 2001).

Sensible project scope management requires that several conditions be met:

- The requirements must be prioritized so that the decision makers can agree upon the capabilities to include in the next release and can evaluate change requests against the priorities of unimplemented requirements in the current baseline.

- The size of the requirements must be evaluated so that the team has an approximate idea of how much effort it will take to implement them.

- The team must know its average productivity so that it can judge how many requirements (measured in some units of size) it can implement and verify per unit time.

- The impact of change requests needs to be analyzed so that the team has a good understanding of what it will cost to implement each one and what the implications are likely to be for the project.

- The decision makers need to be identified and their decision-making process must be established so that they can efficiently decide to modify the scope when appropriate.

Don't be victimized by the specter of creeping scope or attempt in vain to suppress change. Instead, establish a clear scope definition early in the project and use a practical change control process to cope with the inevitable—and often beneficial—requirements evolution.

Chapter 18
The Line in the Sand

Software developers often want to freeze the requirements following some initial requirements development work and then proceed with design and construction, unencumbered with those pesky changes. This is the classic waterfall paradigm. It doesn't work well in most situations. It's far more realistic to define a requirements baseline and then manage changes to that baseline.

Baseline is a term from the domain of configuration management. The IEEE Standard Glossary of Software Engineering Terminology defines it as the following (1990):

> *A specification or product that has been formally reviewed and agreed on, that thereafter serves as the basis for further development, and that can be changed only through formal change control procedures.*

A baseline is given a unique name so that the project participants can refer to it by name and review exactly what elements a previous baseline included. Good configuration management practices allow the team to reconstruct accurately any previous baseline and all its components.

In a broad sense, any approved set of requirements could be defined as a baseline, even before release planning has been done. In this chapter, though, we will think of a requirements baseline as being a snapshot in time that represents the current agreed-upon, reviewed, and approved set of requirements committed to a specific product release. That "release" could be a complete delivered product or any defined, interim increment of the product. The baseline also includes supporting documentation, such as the scope definition that was used to establish the set of committed requirements, information about who approved the baseline, and key source documents for the requirements. When stakeholders "sign off" on requirements, what they're really doing is agreeing and committing to a specific requirements baseline. See Chapter 2 of *Software Requirements, Second Edition* for more recommendations on the requirements approval or sign-off process.

Once the project team establishes a requirements baseline, the team should follow a pragmatic change control process to make good business and technical decisions about adding newly requested functionality and altering or deleting existing requirements. Change control is not about stifling change. It's about providing decision makers with the information that will let them make timely and appropriate decisions to modify the planned functionality. That planned functionality is the baseline.

The Requirements Baseline

Whereas the scope definition distinguishes what's in from what's out, the requirements baseline explicitly identifies those requirements that the project will implement. That is, the baseline is a precise description of what is in scope, but it doesn't identify what is left out. The techniques described in Chapter 17, "Defining Project Scope," provide high-level descriptions of the release contents. The detailed baseline description consists of an explicitly identified set of functional requirements committed for the release.

Where does the baseline live? It's not a tangible item but rather a defined list of items. One possible storage location is a software requirements specification written in the form of a word-processing document. If that SRS contains only the requirements for a specific product release and it indeed contains *all* the requirements for that release, the SRS constitutes the requirements baseline for the release. However, the SRS might include additional requirements that are intended for a later release. (See Chapter 20, "Handling Requirements for Multiple Releases.") Conversely, perhaps multiple software, hardware, and interface specification documents are needed to fully define the components of the baseline. It's essential that the project stakeholders have a clear understanding of exactly what is intended to go into the upcoming release.

But perhaps you're storing your requirements in a requirements management tool or in some other database, rather than in the form of documents. In that case, you can define a baseline as a specific subset of the requirements stored in the database that are planned for a given release. Storing requirements in a tool allows you to maintain an aggregated set of both currently committed requirements and planned future requirements. Some commercial requirements management tools include a baselining function to distinguish those requirements (even down to the specific version of each requirement, perhaps) that belong to a certain baseline.

Alternatively, you could define a requirement attribute to hold the release number or other baseline identifier. Moving a requirement from one baseline to another is then a simple matter of changing the value for that requirement attribute. The attribute approach will work when each requirement belongs to only a single requirements baseline. However, you might well allocate the same requirement (or different versions of the same requirement) to several baselines if you're concurrently developing multiple versions of your product. Tool support is essential for this type of complex baseline management.

Note that you need not baseline all the requirements for the entire product at once. When following an incremental or iterative development life cycle, the baseline for each iteration will represent just a fraction of the overall system's functionality. A small project my team once worked on took this approach. The developer (who also served as project manager, analyst, and tester) worked in three-week cycles. For each cycle, he specified the requirements that were to be designed, coded, verified, and integrated during the next three weeks. Each requirements baseline was therefore quite small. The product grew incrementally toward full functionality as the developer released useful versions periodically to the users.

When to Baseline

Analysts sometimes struggle with exactly when to define a baseline for their requirements. It's an important decision because establishing the baseline has the following implications:

- **Formal change control begins.**   Change requests are made against an established baseline. The baseline therefore provides the point of reference for each proposed change. Make sure your change control process and players are in place before you define any project baselines.

- **Project managers determine the staffing levels and budgets needed.**   There are five dimensions to a software project that must be managed: features, quality, schedule, staff, and budget (Wiegers 1996).[1] Once the features and quality goals are established in the baseline, the project manager manipulates the other three dimensions to see what it will take to accomplish the project's objectives. It can work the other way, too. If staff, budget, and schedule are pre-established by external forces, the baseline composition is necessarily constrained to fit inside the project box bounded by those limits.

- **Project managers make schedule commitments.**   Prior to baselining, requirements are still volatile and uncertain, so estimates are similarly volatile and uncertain. Once a baseline is established, the contents of the release should be sufficiently well understood so that managers can make realistically achievable commitments. The managers still need to accommodate the likelihood of requirements growth by including sensible contingency buffers in their committed schedules.

Baselining requirements too early can push your change control process into overdrive. If the requirements are still evolving and many new requirements are still being identified, you can devote an undue amount of effort to handling changes formally. In fact, receiving a storm of change requests after defining a baseline could be a clue that your requirements elicitation activities were incomplete and perhaps ineffective.

On the other hand, waiting too long to establish a baseline could be a sign of analysis paralysis. Perhaps the analysts are trying too hard to perfect the set of requirements before handing them to the development team for implementation.

---

1. Some people add other dimensions, such as risk. The important concept is to avoid the overly simplistic "iron triangle" approach, which considers only three of these dimensions—most commonly scope, time, and resources, although exactly which three varies from author to author. The iron triangle makes assumptions about which dimensions are static (typically features or quality) and which can be combined (typically features + quality = "scope," or staff + budget = "resources"). In reality, all five of these dimensions can be adjusted and traded off against one another.

Remember, requirements development attempts to define a set of requirements that is not perfect but is *good enough* to let the team proceed with construction at an acceptable level of risk. Unfortunately, no convenient green light comes on to signify when you've reached this point. Instead, use the checklist in Table 18-1 to judge when you're ready to define a requirements baseline as a solid foundation for continuing the product development effort.

Table 18-1   Factors to Consider Before Defining a Requirements Baseline

Business Rules	Determine whether you've identified the business rules that affect the system and whether you've specified functional requirements to enforce or comply with those rules.
Change Control	Make sure a practical change control process is in place for dealing with requirement changes and that the change control board, or CCB, is assembled and chartered. Ensure that the change control tool you plan to use is in place and configured and that the tool users have been trained.
Customer Perspective	Check back with your key customer representatives to see whether their needs have changed since you last spoke. Have new business rules come into play? Have existing rules been modified? Have priorities changed? Have new customers with different needs been identified? Has marketing made any promises that the analysts haven't heard about yet?
Interfaces	See if functionality has been defined to handle all identified external interfaces to users, other software systems, hardware components, and communications services.
Model Validation	Examine any analysis models with the user representatives, perhaps by walking through test cases, to see if a system based on those models would let the users perform their necessary activities.
Prototypes	If you created any prototypes, did appropriate customers evaluate them? Was the knowledge gained used to revise the requirements specification?
Requirements Alignment	Perform a reality check against the project's business objectives to see if the defined set of requirements would likely achieve those objectives. Look for alignment between the business requirements, user requirements, and functional requirements.
Requirements Reviews	Have several downstream consumers of the requirements review them. These consumers include designers, programmers, testers, documentation writers, help system designers, user interface designers, and anyone else who will base their own work on the requirements. Conduct this sort of review activity in an incremental and ongoing fashion. Don't wait until you think the requirements are complete before you ask some people to judge whether they could execute their part of the work based on those requirements.
Scope	Check whether all the requirements being contemplated for the baseline lie within the project scope as it is currently defined. The scope might have changed since it was originally defined early in the project.
TBDs	Scan the documents for TBDs (details yet to be determined) that indicate gaps remaining in the requirements knowledge. Baselining requirements that still contain TBDs increases the uncertainty level in the document. The TBDs represent requirements development work remaining to be done.

Table 18-1   Factors to Consider Before Defining a Requirements Baseline (Continued)

Templates	Examine the document templates you're using to store your various types of requirements. Make sure that each section of the specification has been populated or that an indication has been supplied that that section does not apply to this project. (One example might be, "No constraints have been identified for this project.") Common oversights in the templates are quality attribute requirements, constraints, and assumptions.
User Classes	See whether you've received input from appropriate representatives of all the user classes you've identified for the product.
Verifiability	Determine how you would judge whether each requirement was properly implemented. User acceptance criteria are helpful for this.

You're never going to get perfect, complete requirements. You're never going to know the perfect time to declare a requirements baseline and move on with the project. However, the analyst can use the practices in this chapter to judge whether the requirements are converging toward a product description that will satisfy some defined portion of customer needs and is achievable within the known project constraints. Establishing a baseline at that point establishes a mutual agreement and expectation among the project stakeholders regarding the product they're going to have when they're done. Without such an agreed-upon baseline, there's a good chance someone will be surprised by the outcome of the project. Software surprises are rarely good news.

Chapter 19
The Six Blind Men and the Requirements

There's an old fable from India about six blind men who encountered an elephant for the first time. Although they couldn't see it, they wanted to learn what an elephant was like. Each of them touched a different part of the elephant. The first man grasped the elephant's leg and said, "Why, an elephant is just like a big tree." "No," said the man who was holding the elephant's tail, "an elephant is like a rope." The third man felt the side of the elephant and reported, "This elephant is like a big wall." The fourth man gripped the elephant's trunk and declared, "You're all wrong. The elephant is like a giant snake." The fifth man took hold of the elephant's tusk and said, "I think an elephant resembles a spear." "No, no, no!" said the final man, who touched the elephant's ear. "An elephant is like a big fan."

The blind men were all correct. The elephant has all the characteristics they described, but no single feature of the elephant provides a complete description of what an elephant is all about. Each man had but a limited view of the elephant and could draw conclusions only from that view.

There's an analogy with software requirements. I learned long ago that no single view of the requirements tells us everything we need to know about them (Davis 1995). Often it's desirable to represent requirements in multiple ways, thereby giving the readers a richer, more holistic understanding of the requirements elephant. Unfortunately, nearly every require-ments specification I read contains just one view: natural language text. The adroit analyst can do better than that.

Limitations of Natural Language

Natural language is, well, natural for people to use. We use it every day of our lives in diverse forms. But natural language has some shortcomings. One of the biggest limitations is ambigu-ity. For example, I once was talking with my father about cars. I said, "For my next car, I'd like to get one of those high-mileage gas-electric hybrids." My father replied, "I don't know if you're going to be able to find a used one." Used one? I didn't say anything about buying a used car. When I said *high mileage*, I meant, "gets many miles per gallon." When my father heard *high mileage*, he thought, "big number on the odometer." These are both perfectly sensible interpre-tations of the phrase *high mileage*. Ordinary, natural language led to a miscommunication in a casual discussion with someone I knew quite well.

In conversation, we rely on context, body language, and the chance to ask questions for clarification to ensure that we understand what we heard. We have an opportunity during discussions to detect and quickly correct ambiguity. Written communication, such as a requirements specification, doesn't allow for this opportunity. Confusion can result from misinterpretations and ambiguity. This is one reason why you should never expect an SRS to replace conversations among analysts, developers, and customer representatives. Ambiguity is one of the big risks that natural language poses to high-quality requirements.

Writing in natural language also leads to bulky and verbose specifications. In an attempt to clarify what he's trying to say, the analyst might repeat a piece of information or state it in more than one way. Redundancy is often not helpful in requirements specifications and can introduce additional ambiguities and inconsistencies. And frankly, long specification docu-ments with page after page of text are boring to read and daunting to review. There's a good chance that your reviewers will glaze over and fail to find some of the problems in the docu-ment. (See Chapter 8, "Two Eyes Aren't Enough.")

Another issue is that detailed textual requirement statements represent a low level of abstrac-tion. Each requirement describes but a small fragment of the system's functionality or charac-teristics. Specification readers can have a hard time grasping the big picture and seeing how each individual requirement contributes to it. This makes it difficult for them to judge whether each requirement is correct, complete, and necessary.

Some Alternative Requirements Views

An effective requirements analyst can choose the most appropriate way to represent informa-tion in a given situation. Besides the traditional default of writing natural language requirement statements, the analyst should determine when a picture or some other representation would be valuable. Following are some of the alternative types of requirements views to consider.

Graphical Analysis Models

Table 19-1 lists several of the analysis models[1] that are available to the requirements analyst. Some of these date back to the structured analysis movement of the 1970s and 1980s (Robertson and Robertson 1994). Others are part of the Unified Modeling Language, which provides a rich set of conventions for object-oriented analysis and design (Booch, Rumbaugh, and Jacobson 1999). These models present information visually, not just in the form of text. Chapter 11 of *Software Requirements, Second Edition* describes and provides examples of several of these modeling notations.

Table 19-1   Some Graphical Analysis Models for Representing Requirements

Information Depicted	Structured Analysis	Object-Oriented Analysis
System external interfaces	Context diagram	Use case diagram
Process flow steps	Data flow diagram	Activity diagram
	Flowchart	Swimlane diagram
		Sequence diagram
Data or object interrelationships	Entity-relationship diagram	Class diagram
		Collaboration diagram
		Object diagram
System states or object statuses	State-transition diagram	Statechart diagram
User interface architecture	Dialog map	N/A

Decision Tables and Decision Trees

These are tabular and graphical techniques, respectively, for representing complex logical expressions (such as a sequence of if/then statements) and the associated system behaviors (Wiegers 2003a).

Test Cases

Functional requirements describe the behavior of the software to be built. Test cases describe ways to determine if the correct requirements have been implemented properly. Functional requirements and test cases represent two complementary ways of thinking about the software system. The first is from a constructive perspective (let me try to make it), and the second is from a destructive perspective (let me try to break it). One school of thought in software development maintains that detailed written requirements aren't necessary; acceptance tests provide an adequate description of what needs to be built. I prefer to think of specifications and test cases as being complementary views of the requirements. Thinking about the system from these two perspectives often reveals inconsistencies and gaps in the analyst's knowledge.

---

1. Some authors use the term *model* to describe any technique for representing requirements information, including a list of textual functional requirements. When I say *model* or *analysis model*, I'm referring to some type of drawing or diagram that represents requirements information visually, generally at a higher level of abstraction than detailed functional requirements offer.

Prototypes and Screen Designs

When prototyping, the analyst is taking a tentative step from the requirements domain into the solution space. A prototype is like an experiment. It tests the hypothesis that the requirements you have developed to date are accurate and complete. Most people find it more insightful to work with a prototype than to read through a long list of functional requirements. A prototype serves as a tangible first cut at some portion of the possible product.

A low-resolution prototype provides the gist of the proposed user interface, whereas a high-resolution prototype presents detailed screen designs. However, a visual prototype does not depict the details hidden behind the presentation layer. A prototype doesn't show input field interactions or describe how the system processes input stimuli to produce output responses. As with analysis models, a prototype is an insufficient means of "documenting" requirements; you still need to record the details somewhere.

Tables and Structured Lists

If multiple requirements will be worded similarly except for a particular change from one requirement to the next, consider grouping them in the form of a table or a structured list (Wiegers 2003a). Grouped requirements are more maintainable because a global wording change need be made only once. This is more concise than writing out all the individual requirements in detail, and the differences between the similar requirements will be obvious. For traceability purposes, each item in a list should receive a unique identifier. Following is a set of similar requirements from an actual SRS, shown in the original style and then as a structured list.

Before:

> *SGML.Insert.23: The product shall provide a facility that will insert SGML data corresponding to signature block formats selected by the user from among a set of available boilerplate signature blocks.*

> *SGML.Insert.24: The product shall provide a facility that will insert SGML data corresponding to leaveout formats selected by the user from among a set of available boilerplate leaveouts.*

> *SGML.Insert.25: The product shall provide a facility that will insert SGML data corresponding to caption formats selected by the user from among a set of available boilerplate captions.*

After:

> *SGML.Insert: The product shall provide a facility that will insert SGML data selected by the user from among a set of available boilerplate formats for the following:*

> *.23: Signature blocks*

> *.24: Leaveouts*

> *.25: Captions*

Mathematical Expressions

Mathematics provides a precise, concise, and unambiguous way to represent certain types of requirements information, particularly those associated with performing computations. Some types of computational information are best represented in the form of tables. Two examples are interest rates as a function of investment bond term and discount percentages applied to volume purchases of a product.

Why Create Multiple Views?

If you create only one view of the requirements, you must believe it. You have no other choice. If you create multiple views, though, you can compare them to look for disconnects that reveal errors or different interpretations. There's an old saying:[2] "When the map and the terrain differ, believe the terrain." Unfortunately, we have no absolute terrain for requirements; every representation is a map. Even though you can't tell which representation is correct, differences between them indicate problems.

Consider Figure 19-1. A use case presents a high-level view of requirements from the user's perspective. A primary objective of the use case technique is to help the analyst identify the functional requirements that are needed to let users perform a use case. These functional requirements represent a second, more detailed view. The analyst might also create graphical models that represent additional views of the requirements. The analyst should be able to link the functional requirements with elements shown in the models to make sure these complementary views are in agreement.

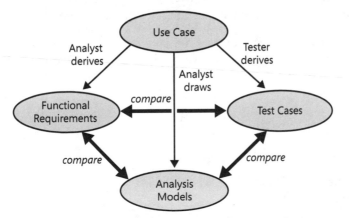

Figure 19-1   Deriving multiple requirements views from a use case.

Suppose a tester were to write some test cases—yet another view—based on the use case. Now the analyst can compare the test cases with the functional requirements and with the analysis

2. Variously attributed to the Swedish Army, the Swiss Army, the Norwegian Boy Scouts, a Scottish prayer, and a Scandinavian proverb.

models to look for mismatches. You might find that a particular test case cannot be executed with the current set of functional requirements. Or you might discover that a specific functional requirement is not covered by any of the test cases. These disconnects can reveal missing requirements, unnecessary requirements, missing test cases, and incorrect test cases. Ambiguities, assumptions, or missing information in the use case description can lead the analyst and the tester to different conclusions, which are revealed only by comparing the various views derived from the use case.

Pictures, such as graphical analysis models, represent information at a higher level of abstraction than detailed text. It's often valuable to step back from the trees and see the forest as a whole—the big picture. This is one way to find those elusive missing requirements. Missing requirements are hard to spot precisely because they don't exist. A reviewer could examine two pages of detailed functional requirements that describe the behavior of some object that can take on multiple statuses, such as a cafeteria meal order or a job application, but he might never detect the one requirement that isn't there.

Suppose, however, you draw a picture—a model—of that aspect of the system using boxes and arrows to show how the object's status can change under certain conditions. This type of model is called a *state-transition diagram*, or *statechart diagram*. The reviewer might immediately notice that a line from one box to another is absent, thereby detecting that missing requirement. The reviewer might also see that a line that goes from box A to box B should be drawn from box A to box C instead. The difference between what the picture shows and the reviewer's mental image of the system provides a way to catch requirement omissions and errors.

This high level of abstraction allows the reader to see how pieces of information fit together without getting mired in the gory details immediately. Of course, developers and testers eventually will need the details so that they can do their jobs. Use high-abstraction models to supplement—not replace—the detailed text with an alternative communication vehicle.

Different people learn and comprehend information in different ways. Some people like to read, others prefer pictures, while still others learn best by listening or while manipulating something with their hands. To accommodate these different learning styles, try to depict information in a variety of ways. It's not obvious how to help tactile learners examine a requirements specification, but multimedia can provide a rich communication experience. Consider embedding hyperlinks in a word-processing document to other types of objects:

- Sound clips that explain a particular concept.
- Video clips that illustrate how something works.
- Photographs that depict views of an object from various angles.

I see little use of hypertext in the requirements documents I review, yet hypertext is an excellent way to provide your readers with easy access to other related information. Consider incorporating links to reusable sources of common data definitions, user class and actor descriptions, glossary entries, business rules, and the like.

Selecting Appropriate Views

There is no single correct way to document specific requirements information. In many situations, structured natural language text is indeed the best approach. Every analyst needs a rich tool kit of techniques at his disposal so that he can choose the most effective requirements view in each situation.

Often, it's valuable to represent information at both high and low levels of abstraction. The high level offers a big-picture perspective, whereas the low level of abstraction presents the nitty-gritty details. For instance, in Chapter 11, "When Use Cases Aren't Enough," I showed a fragment of an event-response table to describe the detailed behavior of a complex highway intersection. A state-transition (or statechart) diagram provides a high-abstraction view of such a system. It shows the various states the system could be in at a given time, the permitted transitions between states, and the conditions that lead to each transition. Both views are necessary to provide a complete understanding of the requirements elephant.

Table 19-2 suggests techniques that are appropriate for representing various types of information at both high and low levels of abstraction. The details of these representation and modeling techniques are beyond the scope of this book. Chapter 11 of *Software Requirements, Second Edition* provides more details on many of these methods and contains references to additional sources to learn about these techniques.

Table 19-2   Choosing the Most Appropriate Requirements Views

Information Depicted	Representation Techniques
System external interfaces	■ The **context diagram** and **use case diagram** identify the objects outside the system that connect to the system. The context diagram illustrates the system inputs and outputs at a high level of abstraction.
	■ External interface details can be recorded in **format descriptions** for input and output files, or **report layouts**. Products that include both software and hardware components often write **interface specifications** with data attribute definitions, perhaps in the form of an application programming interface or specific input and output signals for a hardware device.
Business process flow	■ A top-level **data flow diagram** represents a business process at a high level of abstraction. **Swimlane diagrams** show the roles that participate in executing the various steps in a business process flow.
	■ Refined levels of **data flow diagrams** or **swimlane diagrams** can represent business process flows in considerable detail. Similarly, **flowcharts** and **activity diagrams** can be used at either high or low levels of abstraction, although most commonly they are used to define the details of a process.
	■ A natural language **procedure description** provides the greatest business process detail.

Table 19-2   Choosing the Most Appropriate Requirements Views (Continued)

Information Depicted	Representation Techniques
Data definitions and data object relationships	■ The **entity-relationship diagram** shows the logical relationships between data objects (entities). **Class diagrams** show the logical connections between object classes and the data associated with them.
	■ The **data dictionary** contains detailed definitions of data structures and individual data items. The data dictionary is hierarchical, so it can include high-level entries, such as the flows shown on a context diagram or complex data structures. These items can be progressively broken down into their constituent data elements.
System states	■ **State-transition diagrams** and **statechart diagrams** represent a high-abstraction view of the states a system can be in and changes between states that can take place under certain circumstances.
	■ Some analysts create an **event-response table** as a scoping tool (high abstraction), identifying external events that help define the product's scope boundary.
	■ Alternatively, you can specify individual functional requirements (low abstraction) with an **event-response table** by detailing exactly how the system should behave in response to each combination of external event and system state.
Behavior of an object that can take on multiple statuses	■ The **state-transition diagram** and **statechart diagram** show the possible statuses of the object and the permissible changes from one status to another. These models are helpful when multiple use cases can manipulate (and change the status of) the objects.
	■ **Functional requirements** provide the details that describe exactly what user and system behaviors lead to status changes.
Complex logic	■ A **decision tree** shows the possible outcomes from a set of related true/false decisions or conditions.
	■ A **decision table** identifies the unique functional requirements associated with the various combinations of true and false outcomes for a series of decisions or conditions.
User interfaces	■ The **dialog map** provides a high-level view of a proposed or actual user interface, showing the various display elements (for example, screens and dialog boxes) and possible navigation pathways between them.
	■ **Storyboards** and **low-resolution prototypes** flesh out the dialog map by showing what each screen will contain without depicting precise details.
	■ **Detailed screen layouts** and **high-resolution prototypes** show exactly what the display elements will look like. **Data field definitions** and **user interface control descriptions** provide additional detail.

Table 19-2 Choosing the Most Appropriate Requirements Views (Continued)

Information Depicted	Representation Techniques
User task descriptions	■ **User stories**, **scenarios**, and **use case specifications** describe user tasks in various levels of specificity.
	■ **Sequence diagrams** illustrate the interplay between multiple actors and the system during execution of a use case. **Flowcharts** and **activity diagrams** visually depict the flow of the use case dialog and branches into alternative flows and exceptions.
	■ **Functional requirements** provide detailed descriptions of how the system and user will interact to achieve valuable outcomes.
	■ **Test cases** provide an alternative low-abstraction view, describing exactly what system behavior to expect under specific conditions of inputs, system state, and actions.
Nonfunctional requirements (quality attributes, constraints)	■ Quality attributes and constraints are usually written in the form of **structured text**, but that often results in a lack of precision and completeness. The definitive technique for precisely specifying nonfunctional requirements is **Planguage** (Gilb 2005).

Reconciling Multiple Views

As with every other requirements engineering technique, creating multiple requirements views incurs a cost. In addition to expending effort to create the different views, the analyst must keep them all current as changes are made. If the views get out of sync with each other, readers won't know which one to believe (if any). This reduces the value of the different views. You might not need to update a high-level model every time you change some detailed functionality description, but you'll probably need to revise the corresponding test cases. Don't become a slave to the modeling, caught in the analysis paralysis trap of endlessly perfecting the pictures. In many cases, though, the cost of creating and maintaining multiple views is more than outweighed by the insights into the requirements that different views offer and the errors they reveal.

Part VII
On Managing Requirements

Whatever collection of requirements information your team accumulates must be stored and managed throughout the course of the project. Part VII addresses some specific aspects of managing these requirements. Chapter 20, "Handling Requirements for Multiple Releases," deals with the perplexing matter of concurrently working with sets of requirements that are intended for various future product versions. Several options are presented with their advantages and shortcomings. Chapter 21, "Business Requirements and Business Rules," addresses these two types of requirements information, which are often confused.

Chapter 22, "Measuring Requirements," proposes some basic metrics that can help you get a handle on what's happening with your requirements engineering process. These metrics address the standard software measurement categories of size, effort, quality, and status. The book concludes with Chapter 23, "Exploiting Requirements Management Tools," which offers several recommendations for how to get the most from your investment in these tools. Requirements management tools provide a multitude of capabilities that overcome the deficiencies of document-based requirements specification, but too many organizations fail to use such tools to their best advantage.

Chapter 20
Handling Requirements for Multiple Releases

Software products are rarely delivered in final form with the first release. More commonly, they evolve through a series of releases that correct defects, add progressively more features, and enrich or update previously implemented features. This means that during requirements development you'll be accumulating requirements that could be targeted for various releases. You need to determine the best way to store and manage these requirements so that no one is confused about the contents of each upcoming release.

A related issue pertains to requirements that were proposed but never approved. Similarly, you might approve certain requirements for a specific release, only to delete them later (perhaps deferring them to a future release) either because they are no longer valuable or because of time and resource limitations. Deleted requirements, rejected requirements, ideas, and potential requirements for the future have a way of resurfacing before the project is finished. You don't want to lose sight of the fact that these requirements once were proposed or considered to be in scope. Nor do you want anyone to work on them under the mistaken belief that they're intended for the next release.

There are several ways to handle situations in which you have to deal with requirements that are not a part of the product release the team currently is building. You need to choose the approach that will be the most effective and manageable for your organization's culture and in your development environment. The goal is to produce specifications that clearly identify the requirements for each release, while still providing access to all requirements that describe the historical and possible future states of the product. This chapter compares three strategies for solving this problem:

- Storing all requirements in a single SRS.
- Creating a separate SRS for each release.
- Storing requirements in a requirements management tool.

Single Requirements Specification

One option is to begin by writing an SRS that contains just those requirements that are planned for the initial product release. This approach makes sense if you have a team of people that is continuously working on the next set of prioritized requirements and modifications, creating a release whenever they have a bundle of enhancements and changes ready to go. When you think the initial SRS is complete, define it as a baseline for that first release. (See Chapter 18, "The Line in the Sand.") Store the baselined SRS document in a version control tool, such as those used to manage source code files.[1] Then use check-in and check-out procedures to make changes to the SRS and maintain a revision history of changes made.

As you identify new requirements for any planned release or modify any of the current requirements, highlight those changes using your word processor's revision marks feature. Indicate the planned release number for each requirement in the form of a requirement attribute. This attribute is essential so that the people who will be working from the SRS will know which requirements are in scope for the current release. Also, explicitly identify those requirements that have been deleted or that were proposed once but not approved, along with an explanation of why each decision was made. This retains those requirements for possible future use without allocating them to a particular baseline.

After you've recorded all the requirements you intend to implement in the next release, take the following actions:

1. Archive the SRS in the version control tool, with the revision marks included to identify changes made since the previous version of the document was baselined.

2. Create a copy of the marked-up file. Accept all the revisions, thereby making all the requirements and changes made to them current. Save that version in your version control tool, too. Identify this document as now representing the full set of requirements for the specified product release, including all functionality that was implemented in previous releases. In addition, the document might well include some requirements that are intended for future releases.

3. Continue the process of entering changes with revision marks turned on and periodically baselining the SRS for each subsequent release.

This approach results in developing a single master SRS that contains all the requirements that fully describe your product as it grows through multiple releases. The revision marks in any single historical version represent just the deltas from the previous version.

Creating a master SRS provides the advantage of collecting all the requirements in a single place. New requirements, such as those that enhance previously implemented features, are placed in context wherever they belong. It's also easy to handle requirements that were

---

1. Links to information about many commercial version control tools are available at *http://www.snuffybear.com/ ucmcentral_new_vendorlinks.htm.*

originally planned for a future release but have moved into scope for the current release, perhaps because of a missed dependency, changing priorities, a change in a business rule, or a shift in the market. Because these requirements are already in the specification document, it's just a matter of indicating that they are now planned for the upcoming release.

The single-spec approach has some shortcomings, though. Unless both the SRS author and its readers are careful, it's easy to get confused about which requirements the developers are supposed to implement in a specific release. In addition, it's difficult to view just the subset of the requirements that describe a specific incremental release. The requirements for multiple releases are all threaded together. Suppose that for release 4 you have 43 modified or additional requirements sprinkled throughout your 90-page master SRS. Developers and testers will need to print the entire document and study the revision marks to figure out exactly what to do. This is inefficient and prone to errors.

Multiple Requirements Specifications

If your organization launches a separate project for each new product release, consider writing a separate SRS for each such release (Figure 20-1). The SRS for the first release should follow a comprehensive SRS template, such as the one described in Chapter 10 of *Software Requirements, Second Edition* and available from *http://www.processimpact.com/goodies.shtml*. Much of this information will remain unchanged for future releases. Some document sections that are likely to be stable are product perspective, user classes and characteristics, operating environment, design and implementation constraints, user documentation, assumptions and dependencies, most external interface requirements, and many quality attributes.

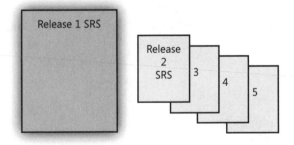

Figure 20-1 Creating a separate SRS for each product release.

Each incremental SRS for a subsequent release will be simpler than the first one, without all the global and background information that appeared in the initial SRS. Each incremental SRS will describe just those functional requirements that are being added or changed. Performance requirements, other quality attributes, and business rules might be associated with specific new or modified functionality, as well. Consider using different document templates for the comprehensive initial SRS and for the smaller and simpler incremental specifications.

If you create multiple specifications in this way, you can use each separate document to describe exactly what the team is going to do in a particular release. This is more reliable than hoping that every reader will correctly glean all the changes from an increasingly massive master SRS. Individual specifications are smaller, less intimidating, and easier to work with, especially in hard copy form.

Naturally, creating multiple specifications presents some disadvantages, too. Shifting a requirement from one planned release to another requires that you physically remove the text describing that requirement from one document and insert it in another. Writing a separate SRS for each release doesn't provide the context and big-picture synthesis of what the whole product is today. Someone who wants to get a complete description of any feature, let alone the entire product, has to assemble bits of information from multiple sources. A compromise strategy is to develop a full specification every two or three releases. That document would aggregate the incremental specifications written since the previous composite document was created into a specification that accurately describes the current product.

When you create multiple specifications, it's also easy to lose track of those requirements that were *not* allocated to a particular product release. There's no logical place to put them, unless you create yet another document to contain the "leftover" requirements that might be of future interest.

Requirements Management Tools

The most robust strategy is to store the requirements in the database of a commercial requirements management tool. This keeps the requirements for all releases stored together. You can use the tool's baseline-definition feature to distinguish those requirements subsets that belong to different releases. Alternatively, you could define a requirement attribute to hold the planned release number for each requirement. Reallocating a requirement from one release to another then becomes a simple matter of changing this attribute. A status attribute helps you distinguish rejected or deleted requirements from the others. You could also define a rationale attribute to describe why a requirement was deleted from a release baseline or why it was never approved. This is valuable in case the requirement comes up for discussion again later on.

When you store requirements in a tool, an SRS becomes a report generated from the database contents according to specific query and filter criteria. You have several options:

- To see a complete specification for the entire product to date, extract all the requirements for the current version and all previous releases.

- To see the specification for a single incremental release, report just the requirements allocated to that release.

- To see the requirements that were proposed but rejected, or those that never made it into the product in the first place, base your query on the appropriate values of the status attribute.

Requirements management tools definitively solve the problem of managing requirements for multiple releases. The tools overcome many of the limitations of document-based storage. For example, some tools will retain all historical versions of every individual requirement, whereas version control tools generally maintain previous versions of entire documents. Commercial requirements management tools let you store requirements in a single master location that is always current and is accessible via the Internet to authorized stakeholders.

Powerful requirements management tools are far more expensive than a simple word processor. But the capabilities they provide outweigh the costs in many situations. You can find descriptions and product feature comparisons of many commercial requirements management tools at *http://www.paper-review.com/tools/rms/read.php* and *http://www.volere.co.uk/tools.htm*. Chapter 23, "Exploiting Requirements Management Tools," discusses these tools in more depth, as does Chapter 23 of *Software Requirements, Second Edition*.

Requirements management tools also provide an advantage if you currently have multiple requirements specifications for different parts of your product. For example, a multitier client/server system might have separate specifications for the presentation layer, the middleware layer, and the back-end server. Correlating different versions of these multiple specification documents is messy unless you lock the pieces together with careful version control and release planning. However, storing all these requirements in a tool's database allows you to use requirement attributes and traceability links to establish the connections between individual elements for the various parts of the overall product.

As with so many of the other thorny issues discussed in this book, there is no perfect and simple solution to the matter of concurrently managing requirements for multiple product releases (or similarly, multiple variations of a single product). It's most important that your project team determine in advance what techniques and tools it will use to deal with this situation, using the strategies described in this chapter as a starting point.

Chapter 21

Business Requirements and Business Rules

As Chapter 1, "Fundamentals of Software Requirements," pointed out, the terminology used when discussing software requirements is the source of much confusion. A frequent perplexity is the difference between a business requirement and a business rule. This chapter describes how I distinguish between these two classes of essential requirements information.

Business Requirements

A *business requirement* states a high-level business objective of the organization that builds a product or an objective of the customer who procures it. Business requirements describe how the world will be better for certain communities of people if this new product is available. Business requirements generally come from the funding sponsor for a project, the acquiring customer, the manager of the actual end users, the marketing department, or a product visionary. These requirements answer an essential question: "Why are we devoting resources to this project?"

Table 21-1 presents some examples of financial and nonfinancial business objectives (Wiegers 2002b). Business objectives fit into the following categories:

- Tangible financial benefits such as reduced costs, enhanced market share, increased revenue, broadening the customer base, or the ability to charge premium prices.

- Improvements in business operations such as specific transaction throughput or accuracy goals, customer satisfaction measures, retiring of legacy applications or technologies, or reduced support and maintenance costs.

- Strategic positioning or brand enhancement the company hopes to achieve with the product.

- Regulatory compliance.

- Competitive positioning with respect to other suppliers' products.

- Technology development or acquisition that provides strategic benefits or leverage for future product development.

Table 21-1 Some Examples of Financial and Nonfinancial Business Objectives

Financial	Nonfinancial
■ Save $X per year by replacing a high-maintenance legacy system.	■ Reduce the average time for a customer to book a cruise on the Web site by 50%.
■ Capture a market share of X% in region Y within Z months.	■ Process at least X transactions per day with at least Y% accuracy.
■ Reach a sales volume of X units or revenue of $Y within Z months.	■ Achieve a customer satisfaction measure of at least X within Y months of release.
■ Reduce support costs by X% within Y months.	■ Release the product to market within X months to provide specified business advantages from that timing.
■ Achieve X% profit or return on investment within Y months. Receive no more than X service calls per unit and Y warranty claims per unit within Z months after shipping.	■ Be rated as the top product for reliability in published product reviews by a specified date.
	■ Reduce turnaround time to X hours on Y% of customer support calls.

Write your business objectives in a precise, quantitative, and verifiable fashion. Vague objectives such as "world class" or "killer app" are meaningless because you can't measure whether you've achieved them.

In addition to stating business objectives, business requirements could include a concise product vision statement, stakeholder profiles, high-level feature descriptions, project priorities, and a statement of product limitations. Well-defined business requirements are not sufficient to let developers know what to build. However, they set the stage for all the project work that follows. The subsequent levels of requirements details—user requirements and functional requirements—must align with achieving the business objectives. I recommend capturing business requirements in a vision and scope document. A template for such a document is available from *http://www.processimpact.com/goodies.shtml* and is described in Chapter 5 of *Software Requirements, Second Edition.*

Business Rules

A *business rule* is a company policy, an industry standard, or a law or government regulation that defines, constrains, or governs some aspect of the business. Most business rules exist independently from a specific software system. For this reason, I recommend that you document your business rules separately from the requirements specification for a particular product. Treat your business rules as an enterprise-level asset, not a project-level asset. This facilitates reusing the rules, as they're likely to apply to multiple projects and products. A business rules catalog is a convenient place to collect the rules that affect your applications if they aren't already documented somewhere else, such as in a body of laws. Several comprehensive books on business rules have been published in recent years (Ross 2003; Morgan 2002; von Halle 2002). See Chapter 9 of *Software Requirements, Second Edition* for more about business rules.

Business rules would apply even if the business processes were being performed manually instead of with the help of software. This is one way to distinguish a rule from a software requirement. As an illustration, I borrow a lot of movies on DVD from my local library. If a movie I want to see isn't available immediately, I put my name on the waiting list and eventually I reach the top of the list. Once when I tried to request a movie, the library's Web site displayed an error message: "Sorry, your library only allows you to have 10 items on reserve at one time. Your reserve list already has 10 items, so you can't reserve this item now." The software was enforcing a library policy—a business rule. That same policy applied long before the library used computers, when librarians kept track of reserve lists manually. The business rule thus has an existence outside the scope of any particular library software application.

Even if you aren't building business applications, your products could be subject to business rules in the form of government regulations and industry standards. Electrical products that contain embedded software might require Underwriters Laboratories certification. To obtain this certification, the products must comply with specific safety standards, which constitute a set of business rules. Products that require certification by government bodies such as the U.S. Food and Drug Administration are subject to business rules in the form of laws and regulations. If your product doesn't conform to the pertinent rules, the federal government won't approve it for sale in the United States.

Business Rules and Software Requirements

I do not regard business rules as being software requirements. Instead, I think of them as the origin of requirements that we need to implement to comply with or enforce the rule. Here's an illustration. Because of recent concerns about privacy of medical records in the United States, healthcare providers are subject to a business rule (in this case, a government regulation) along these lines:

> *Before providing any healthcare services to a patient, a healthcare provider must give the patient a copy of the policy that describes how the provider will protect the privacy of the patient's medical records.*

Again, this rule would apply even if no software were involved. The healthcare provider's office staff would have to hand the patient a copy of the privacy policy before the patient could receive any care and would have to keep records of who has received the privacy policies.

But suppose your team was developing or enhancing the appointment-management software used in doctors' offices and you needed to enforce this new business rule. The requirements analyst for the appointment system could derive a variety of functional requirements to comply with the rule, depending on the situation. Following are some possibilities:[1]

- When a patient calls to make an appointment, if the patient's profile contains an e-mail address and the patient has requested to receive communications by e-mail, the system shall e-mail the patient a PDF file of the privacy policy with return receipt requested. When the system receives a return receipt acknowledging that the e-mail was opened, the system shall record that the privacy policy has been delivered.

- Alternatively, if the patient has not requested to receive communications by e-mail and the patient is not physically present in the office to make the appointment, the system shall issue a request to the Patient Mailing System to mail a printed copy of the privacy policy to the patient. When the Patient Mailing System confirms that the policy has been mailed, the system shall record that the privacy policy has been delivered.

- Or, if the patient is present in the office when making the appointment, the office staff member shall hand the patient a copy of the privacy policy. When the patient signs an acknowledgment of receipt, the office staff member shall record this delivery in the patient's profile.

As this example illustrates, the business rule can lead to various sets of functional requirements—and manual operations—depending on the situation. It's usually not a simple matter of just reiterating the rule and calling it a "requirement." I have seen situations, though, in which the way a functional requirement was written simply restated the business rule, so this can indeed happen. Nevertheless, the business rule is the origin or rationale for the functionality that is generated to comply with the rule. Traceability data is valuable for identifying the origin of functional requirements that the analyst derived from business rules.

Another possibility is that the rule influences exactly how the analyst writes a particular requirement. Suppose you have some requirements that control access to certain functions of your company's information systems through password controls and user privilege levels. Descriptions of which privilege levels are permitted to perform certain operations will be found in your business rules. So the functional requirements for those operations will be included in the specification, and the rules will govern just how the requirements are written to allow only authorized users to perform those operations.

Business rules could also lead to nonfunctional requirements. Figure 21-1 illustrates how this might work. (This example is incomplete; it merely illustrates the point.) A corporate security policy—a business rule—implies the need for certain integrity requirements, a type of quality attribute. The fundamental underlying integrity requirement, or course, is that the system

---

1. These requirements are for illustration purposes only. I do not mean to imply that they are the correct way, or the only way, to comply with this sample business rule. Nor do these examples deal with issues such as the e-mail recipient suppressing the return receipt request. Real life is always more complicated than learning examples.

shall validate that a user is who he claims to be within some small probability of error. The integrity requirements given as examples in Figure 21-1 are intended to help achieve this objective from a practical point of view. (Remember, one person's "what" is another person's "how.") The security policy and the integrity requirements lead the analyst to derive functional requirements that will enforce that policy and satisfy those integrity requirements.

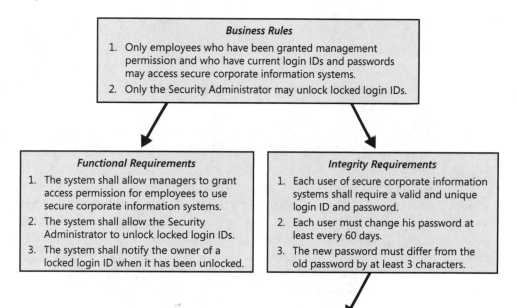

Figure 21-1   Links between business rules, quality attributes, and functional requirements.

Note the reuse opportunities provided by broadly applicable business rules and the other requirements derived from them. Reuse at a high level of abstraction—the requirements level—provides greater opportunities for increasing productivity than does code-level reuse. Reuse also facilitates commonality and consistency across applications.

Another category of business rules has to do with how computations are performed. Some computational formulas are dictated by corporate policies, such as:

- Product discounts for volume purchases or preferred customers.

- Insurance premiums.

- Shipping costs.

- Airline ticket fares (these involve highly complex and proprietary rules).

Other types of computational rules are established by government regulations. Examples include income and sales tax calculations, overtime pay, and Social Security benefits. It's often clearer to represent computations in the form of mathematical formulas or tables, rather than using natural language text.

Some projects use computational algorithms that reflect the professional judgment of the developers but are not really obligatory. Algorithms chosen for the purpose of implementing some specific product functionality, such as searching data or solving mathematical equations, are not business rules. They aren't requirements, either. Instead, they're an aspect of design, in that the developer has selected a particular numerical technique to address a set of requirements, such as calculating a spacecraft trajectory to a certain accuracy level and within a specified length of time. Computations based on laws of nature or physics are neither business rules nor requirements, just design choices. However, if the algorithm to use is dictated rather than left to the developer's discretion, this constitutes an imposed design constraint, which *is* a type of requirement.

An easy way to distinguish a business rule from a requirement is to ask whether the statement in question would still apply if the process it addresses were being performed manually. If so, that statement is most likely a business rule. But if not, the statement probably is a software requirement.

Chapter 22
Measuring Requirements

Disciplined software organizations collect a focused set of metrics about each of their projects. These metrics provide insight into the size of the product; the effort, time, and money that the project or individual tasks consumed; the project status; and the product's quality. Because requirements are an essential project component, you should measure several aspects of your requirements development and management activities (Costello and Liu 1995; Wiegers 2001). An effective technique for choosing the right metrics for your organization is called *goal-question-metric*, or GQM (Basili and Rombach 1988). GQM is a structured thought process that helps you identify the metrics that will answer questions about whether your teams are achieving project and organizational goals.

Product Size

The most fundamental metric is the number of requirements in a body of work. Your project might represent requirements by using a mix of use cases, functional requirements, feature descriptions, business rules, event-response tables, and analysis models. However, the team implements functional requirements. Begin your requirements measurement by simply counting the individual functional requirements that are allocated to the baseline for a given product release. If different team members can't count the requirements and get the same answer, you have to wonder what other sorts of ambiguities and misunderstandings they'll experience. Knowing how many requirements are going into a release will help you judge how the team is progressing toward completion because you can monitor the backlog of work remaining to be done. If you don't know how many requirements you need to work on, how will you know when the project is done?

It's true that not all functional requirements are the same size or consume the same implementation and testing effort. If you're going to count functional requirements as an indicator of system size, your analysts will need to write them at a consistent level of granularity. One guideline is to decompose high-level requirements until the child requirements are all individually testable (Wilson 1995). That is, a tester can design a few logically related tests to verify whether a requirement was correctly implemented. Count the total number of child requirements because those are what the developers will implement and the testers will test. Alternative requirements sizing techniques include use case points and story points. See Chapter 5, "Estimating Based on Requirements," for details about these measures of size.

Functional requirements are not the whole story, of course. Stringent nonfunctional requirements can consume considerable design and implementation effort. Some functional requirements are derived from specified nonfunctional requirements, so those would be incorporated into the functional requirement size estimate. But not all nonfunctional requirements will be reflected in this size estimate. Consider the following situations:

- If the user must have multiple ways to access specific functions to improve usability, more development effort will be necessary than if only one access mechanism is needed, even though the same functional requirements are being implemented in both cases.

- Imposed design and implementation constraints, such as multiple external interfaces to achieve compatibility with an existing operating environment, can lead to a lot of interface work even though no additional new product functionality is added.

- Extensive algorithm and database design work could be needed to satisfy strict performance requirements, whereas less effort might be needed to implement the same functionality in a less severely constrained environment.

- Rigorous availability and reliability requirements can imply significant work to build in failover and data recovery mechanisms.

For these reasons, be sure to consider the impact of nonfunctional requirements upon the effort you estimate it would take to implement the defined functional requirements. The team's productivity might be lower than expected if they have to expend a lot of effort to comply with demanding performance, external interface, and quality requirements.

 You'll also find it informative to track the growth in requirements as a function of time, no matter what requirements size metric you use. One of my clients found that their projects typically grew in size by about 25 percent before delivery. They were also about 25 percent over the planned schedule on most of their projects. Coincidence? I think not.

Requirements Quality

Consider collecting some data regarding the quality of your requirements. Inspections of requirements specifications are a good source of this information (Wiegers 2002a). Count the requirements defects you discover and classify them into various categories: missing requirements, erroneous requirements, unnecessary requirements, incompleteness, ambiguities, and so forth. Use defect type frequencies and root cause analysis to tune up your requirements processes so that the team makes fewer of these types of errors in the future. For instance, if you find that missing requirements are a common problem, your elicitation approaches need some adjustments.

If the team members don't think they have time to inspect all their requirements documentation, try inspecting a sample of just a few pages. Then calculate the average defect density (defects found per specification page) for this sample. Assuming that the sample was representative of the entire document (a big assumption), you can multiply the number of uninspected pages by this defect density to estimate the number of undiscovered defects that could still lurk in the specification. Less experienced inspectors might discover only, say, half the defects that actually are present, so use this estimated number of undiscovered defects as a lower bound. Inspection sampling can let you assess the document's quality so that you can determine whether it's cost effective to inspect the rest of the requirements specification (Gilb and Graham 1993). The answer will almost certainly be yes.

Also keep records of requirements defects that are identified after the requirements are baselined, such as requirements-related problems discovered during design, coding, and testing. These represent errors that leaked through your quality control filters during requirements development. Calculate the percentage of the total number of requirements errors that the team caught at the requirements stage. Removing requirements defects early is far cheaper than correcting them after the team has already designed, coded, and tested the wrong requirements. Two informative metrics to calculate from inspection data are *effectiveness* and *efficiency* (Wiegers 2002a):

Effectiveness   The percentage of the defects originally present in a work product that was discovered by inspection.

Efficiency   The average number of defects discovered per labor hour of inspection effort.

Effectiveness will tell you how well your inspections (or other requirements quality techniques) are working. Efficiency will tell you what it costs you, on average, to discover a defect through inspection. You can compare that cost with the cost of dealing with requirements defects found later in the project or after delivery to judge whether improving the quality of your requirements is cost effective.

Requirements Status

Track the status of each requirement over time to monitor overall project status, perhaps defining a requirement attribute to store this information. Status tracking can help you avoid the pervasive "90 percent done" problem of software project tracking. Each requirement will have one of the following statuses at any time. (See Chapter 18 of *Software Requirements, Second Edition*.)[1]

- Proposed (someone suggested it).
- Approved (it was allocated to a baseline).
- Implemented (the code was designed, written, and unit tested).

---

1. Other status options are possible, of course. Some organizations add a status of "Reviewed" because they want to confirm that a requirement is of high quality before allocating it to a baseline. Other organizations add "Delivered to Customer" to indicate that a requirement has actually been released.

- Verified (the requirement passed its tests after integration into the product).

- Deferred (the requirement will be implemented in a future release).

- Deleted (you decided not to implement it at all).

- Rejected (the idea was never approved).

When you ask a developer how he is coming along, he might say, "Of the 87 requirements allocated to this subsystem, 61 of them are verified, 9 are implemented but not yet verified, and 17 aren't yet completely implemented." There's a good chance that not all these requirements are the same size, will consume the same amount of implementation effort, or will deliver the same customer value. It's also possible that the functional requirements that have been verified do not fully implement any use cases, only portions of the use cases from which the functional requirements were derived. If I were a project manager, though, I'd feel that we had a good handle on the size of that subsystem and how close we were to completion. This is far more informative than, "I'm about 90 percent done. Lookin' good!"

Requests for Changes

Much of requirements management involves handling requirement additions, modifications, and deletions. Therefore, track the status and impact of your requirements change requests. The data you collect should enable your team to answer questions such as the following:

- How many change requests were submitted in a given time period?

- How many of these requests are open, and how many are closed?

- How many requests were approved, and how many were rejected?

- How much effort did the team spend implementing each approved change?

- How long have the requests been open on average?

- On average, how many individual requirements or other artifacts are affected by each submitted change request?

- Exactly which requirements were modified in response to each change request? (Use traceability records to keep track of this information.)

Monitor how many changes are incorporated throughout development after you baselined the requirements for a specific release. Note that a single change request potentially can affect multiple requirements of different levels and types: user requirements, functional requirements, and nonfunctional requirements. You can calculate requirements volatility over a given time period by dividing the number of changed requirements by the total number of requirements at the beginning of the period (for example, at the time a baseline was defined):

$$\text{Requirements Volatility} = \frac{\text{added + modified + deleted requirements}}{\text{initial number of requirements}}$$

The intent is not to try to eliminate requirements volatility but to ensure that the project can manage the degree of requirements changes and still meet its commitments. Changes become more expensive as the product nears completion, and a sustained high level of approved change requests makes it difficult to know when you can ship the product. Most projects should become more resistant to making changes as development progresses, meaning the trend of accepted changes should approach zero as you near the planned completion date for a given release. An incremental development approach gives the team multiple opportunities to incorporate changes into subsequent increments, while still keeping each incremental release on schedule.

Receiving many change requests suggests that elicitation overlooked many requirements or that new ideas keep coming in as the project drags along month after month. Record where the change requests come from: marketing, users, sales, testing, management, engineering, and so on. The change request origins will suggest with whom you need to work to reduce the number of overlooked, modified, and misunderstood requirements.

Change requests that remain unresolved for a long time suggest that your change management process isn't working well. I once visited a company where a manager wryly admitted that they had enhancement requests that were several years old and still pending. This team should allocate certain of their open requests to specific planned maintenance releases and convert other long-term deferred change requests to a status of rejected. This would help the project manager focus the team's energy on the most important and most urgent items in the change backlog.

Effort

Finally, record the time your team spends on requirements engineering activities. These activities include both requirements development (getting and writing good requirements) and requirements management (dealing with change, tracking status, recording traceability data, and so on).

I'm frequently asked how much time and effort a project should allocate to these functions. The answer depends enormously on the type and size of project, the developing team and organization, and the application domain. (See Chapter 4, "How Long Do Requirements Take?") If you track your own team's investment in these critical project activities, you can better estimate how much effort to plan for future projects.

Suppose that on one previous project, your team expended 10 percent of its effort on requirements activities. In retrospect, you conclude that the requirements were too poorly defined and the project would have benefited from additional investment in developing quality requirements. The next time your team tackles a similar project, the project manager would be wise to allocate more than 10 percent of the total project effort to the requirements work.

As you accumulate data, correlate the project development effort with some measure of product size. The documented requirements should give you an indication of size. You could correlate effort with the count of individually testable requirements, use case points, function points, or something else that is proportional to product size. As Figure 22-1 illustrates, such correlations provide a measure of your development team's productivity, which will help you estimate and scope individual release contents. If you collect some product size data and track the corresponding implementation effort, you'll be in a better position to create meaningful estimates for similar projects in the future.

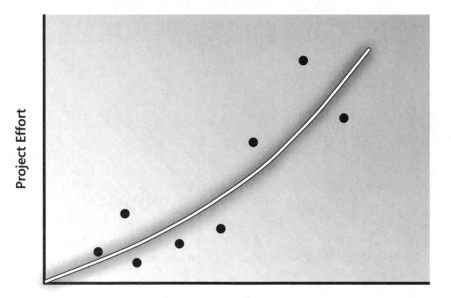

Figure 22-1   Correlating project effort with requirements size gives a measure of team productivity. Each point represents a separate hypothetical project.

Chapter 23

Exploiting Requirements Management Tools

 Several chapters of this book mentioned requirements management tools. More than two dozen such commercial tools are on the market today. They range from simple Web-based structures for storing requirements information to powerful, multiuser, Web-enabled products with rich feature sets that can handle extremely large projects. Chapter 21 of *Software Requirements, Second Edition* describes the general characteristics and capabilities of this class of software tool. Descriptions and comparative information about many of the tools are available at *http://www.paper-review.com/tools/rms/read.php* and *http://www.volere.co.uk/tools.htm*.

Earlier, I pointed out some limitations in using word-processing documents to store requirements. Storing requirements in a database or in one of these commercial tools overcomes many of those limitations. I know of many organizations that have explored using requirements management tools, but few of them have completely made the transition. These tools constitute expensive shelfware in too many software development organizations. This chapter offers some suggestions about how to sensibly integrate requirements management tools into your business and get your money's worth from them.

Write Good Requirements First

It's important to remember that these are requirements *management* tools, not requirements *development* tools. They won't help you define your business objectives, scope your project, identify the right user representatives, ask them the right questions, or write good requirements. The tools are not a substitute for effective requirements development processes and techniques. However, they will help you manage and track whatever information you store in them. It's a classic case of garbage in, garbage out.

Therefore, I do not recommend that organizations adopt a requirements management tool unless their analysts can already write good requirements. I've seen companies gain a false confidence in the quality of their requirements because the requirements were nicely stored in a database, well organized, and accessible through handsome reports. Nice-looking but poor quality requirements don't help you very much.

Expect a Culture Change

Most organizations are accustomed to storing requirements in word-processing documents. They already have mechanisms in place for creating, reviewing, approving, storing, distributing, and modifying these documents. A requirements management tool brings a significant new paradigm to these organizations.

Requirements are ethereal enough already. Being able to print the requirements gives them a slightly more tangible feel. But storing them in the deep, dark recesses of a database makes them even *less* tangible. It seems difficult for organizations to completely make the transition from the familiar document approach to storing requirements only in a database. One trap is investing effort into putting requirements in the tool while still retaining the original documents as the master requirements location. Your goal is to have all stakeholders regard the tool as the ultimate source of the current requirements for their project and not rely on the original requirements documents. This culture change will demand gentle pressure relentlessly applied by the managers and change agents in the organization to steer the organization to the new ways of thinking and working.

Choose a Database-Centric or Document-Centric Tool

When selecting a requirements management tool, think about whether a database-centric or document-centric paradigm will be more effective for your organization. Some tools take a document-centric approach. You connect your word-processing document to the tool, identify specific elements in the document as being discrete requirements, and import those into the tool either automatically or manually. Once those requirements are stored in the tool's database, you can manipulate them in the usual ways: assign attributes, define traceability links, and so forth. However, the database contents must be kept synchronized with the document contents. This synchronization can get clumsy, but it's comfortable for people who are accustomed to working with documents. In addition, supplemental information, such as graphics and tables, needs to remain stored in the word-processing document if the tool can't handle those kinds of objects. This means that users of the requirements must go to multiple locations to get all the information they need about a specific portion of the new product.

The database-centric tools dispense with documents entirely and just treat the contents of the repository as the requirements collection. The more powerful products allow you to store various types of objects in the database, including graphics, as well as maintaining links to objects stored in documents or other files. An SRS then becomes a report generated from the database according to selected query and filtering criteria. The tools that are designed with a database at the center eliminate the clumsy synchronization between document and database that the document-centric tools demand.

Don't Create Too Many Requirement Types or Attributes

Most requirements management tools allow you to define a variety of requirement type, sometimes called *classes*. Figure 23-1 suggests some requirements types to consider defining. Each type can have its own set of *attributes*, pieces of data associated with that requirement type. You might define a use case requirement type that contains the components found in a typical use case template. You could also create a functional requirement type with a different set of attributes. Some attributes to consider for functional requirements are author, priority, status, origin, release number, validation method, rationale, and current owner. The tool will create and update certain attributes automatically, such as the creation date or date of last change. Other attributes are user-defined.

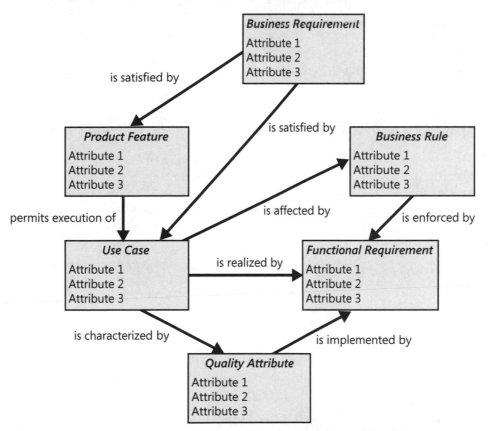

Figure 23-1   Some possible requirement types and potential traceability links.

The arrows in Figure 23-1 illustrate traceability links that you could define to record the logical connections between different types of requirements stored in the tool. All these requirements types, attributes, and traceability connections are potentially valuable. However, don't define any more of these than you really expect to populate and use because it takes effort to create and maintain them. Your team should select the information and traceability links that add value to its projects, and they should be diligent about storing that information and keeping it current.

It's easy to get carried away with designing the requirements database contents instead of thinking about how your team members will actually use the tool and the information stored in it. Instead of defining more attributes than you can manage, I'd rather see you define just three or four attributes initially, populate them, and take good advantage of the data. Priority, status, release number, and rationale comprise a good starter set of attributes for functional requirements.

Train the Tool Users

Although some requirements management tools are inexpensive, the high-end products can represent a significant financial investment. The team members must learn how to use your chosen tool appropriately and efficiently, so don't skimp on training. It's tempting to assume that smart people can figure out how to use any software tool. Spending money on training and support after you've bought expensive licenses can be tough to sell to your managers. But if the participants don't know how to use the tool effectively, you won't get a suitable return on the investment.

Assign Responsibilities

Someone must be responsible for the care and feeding of both the tool and the information stored in it. These are reasonable tasks for the requirements analyst, although the tool administration and content management functions could be split between different people. But the analyst won't be the only person working with the information. You might need to give certain individuals authority to update requirement attributes or to add traceability data during the course of the project. If these responsibilities are not made clear and accepted by the team members, important work won't get done. This degrades the quantity, quality, and value of the data stored in the tool.

For instance, it takes little effort—but considerable discipline—to accumulate traceability information as the software development work is being done. In contrast, it's very expensive or even impractical to assemble all the traceability data at the end of the project. All team members who are in a position to generate traceability data (such as designers, programmers, and testers) must agree to record the traceability links as they do their work.

Take Advantage of Tool Features

 I know of one organization that exported all the requirements for a huge five-year project from their specification documents into a high-end requirements management tool. They defined countless traceability links among the various types of requirements stored in the tool. The only thing they did with all the data, though, was to generate hefty traceability reports. As it happened, no one in the organization actually used these reports. The analysts didn't exploit the other features this powerful tool provided, and the developers still relied on paper specifications as the definitive source of requirements. The investment this organization made in acquiring, installing, configuring, and populating its requirements management tool didn't yield a meaningful return.

Conversely, I know of projects that stored their requirements in a tool but didn't take advantage of any capabilities the tool offered for managing those requirements. One of the strongest arguments for requirements management tools is having the ability to define traceability links. The more robust requirements management products even allow analysts to establish such links to objects stored in other tools, such as to design elements stored in a modeling tool, code segments in a version control tool, and tests in a test management tool. If you don't use the traceability feature, the value of keeping the requirements in a database is diminished.

The tools also let you define groups and individuals with different permission levels to identify who can read, create, and modify the contents of the database. Access controls are an important consideration for companies that have employees in multiple countries. These companies must be careful not to inappropriately expose sensitive technology and data to individuals who do not have the right to see that information. In contrast, information contained in a written document is visible to any reader. Take advantage of these tool capabilities to ensure that all the right people—and only the right people—can access your project's requirements.

Requirements management tools make managing requirements easier, but not easy. Before you invest in such a tool, define your own requirements for it so that your team will select a product that's a good match for its needs. See Chapter 21 of *Software Requirements, Second Edition* for guidance on developing a tool selection process. Don't get caught in the shelfware trap when you look into requirements management tools.

References

Alexander, Ian F., and Neil Maiden, eds. 2004. *Scenarios, Stories, Use Cases: Through the Systems Development Life-Cycle*. Chichester, UK: John Wiley & Sons, Ltd.

Alexander, Ian F., and Richard Stevens. 2002. *Writing Better Requirements*. London: Addison-Wesley.

Ambler, Scott W., and Larry L. Constantine. 2000a. *The Unified Process Inception Phase: Best Practices in Implementing the UP*. Lawrence, KS: CMP Books.

——. 2000b. *The Unified Process Elaboration Phase: Best Practices in Implementing the UP*. Lawrence, KS: CMP Books.

Armour, Frank, and Granville Miller. 2001. *Advanced Use Case Modeling: Software Systems*. Boston: Addison-Wesley.

Basili, Victor R., and H. Dieter Rombach. 1988. "The TAME Project: Towards Improvement-Oriented Software Environments." *IEEE Transactions on Software Engineering* 14(6): 758–773.

Beck, Kent. 2000. *Extreme Programming Explained: Embrace Change*. Reading, MA: Addison-Wesley Longman.

Beck, Kent, and David West. 2004. "User Stories in Agile Software Development." In *Scenarios, Stories, Use Cases: Through the Systems Development Life-Cycle*, ed. Ian F. Alexander and Neil Maiden, 265–279. Chichester, UK: John Wiley & Sons, Ltd.

Beyer, Hugh, and Karen Holtzblatt. 1998. *Contextual Design: Defining Customer-Centered Systems*. San Francisco: Morgan Kaufmann Publishers, Inc.

Bittner, Kurt, and Ian Spence. 2003. *Use Case Modeling*. Boston: Addison-Wesley.

Blackburn, Joseph D., Gary D. Scudder, and Luk N. Van Wassenhove. 1996. "Improving Speed and Productivity of Software Development: A Global Survey of Software Developers." *IEEE Transactions on Software Engineering* 22(12): 875–885.

Boehm, Barry W. 1981. *Software Engineering Economics*. Englewood Cliffs, NJ: Prentice-Hall.

Boehm, Barry W., et al. 1975. "Some Experience with Automated Aids to the Design of Large-Scale Reliable Software." *IEEE Transactions on Software Engineering* 1(1): 125–33.

Booch, Grady, James Rumbaugh, and Ivar Jacobson. 1999. *The Unified Modeling Language User Guide*. Reading, MA: Addison-Wesley.

Brians, Paul. 2003. *Common Errors in English Usage*. Wilsonville, OR: William, James & Company.

Cockburn, Alistair. 2001. *Writing Effective Use Cases*. Boston: Addison-Wesley.

Cohn, Mike. 2004. *User Stories Applied: For Agile Software Development*. Boston: Addison-Wesley.

Cooper, Alan. 1999. *The Inmates Are Running the Asylum: Why High-Tech Products Drive Us Crazy and How to Restore the Sanity*. Indianapolis, IN: Sams.

Costello, Rita J., and Liu, Dar-Biau. 1995. "Metrics for Requirements Engineering." *J. Systems Software* 29(1): 39–63.

Davis, Alan M. 1993. *Software Requirements: Objects, Functions, and States*. Englewood Cliffs, NJ: PTR Prentice Hall.

——. 1995. *201 Principles of Software Development*. New York: McGraw-Hill.

DeMarco, Tom. 1979. *Structured Analysis and System Specification*. Englewood Cliffs, NJ: Prentice-Hall.

——. 2001. *Slack: Getting Past Burnout, Busywork, and the Myth of Total Efficiency*. New York: Broadway Books.

DeMarco, Tom, and Timothy Lister. 1999. *Peopleware: Productive Projects and Teams, Second Edition*. New York: Dorset House Publishing.

Derby, Esther. 2004. "Building a Requirements Foundation Through Customer Interviews." *Insights* 2(1): 1–4.

Fairley, Richard E., and Mary Jane Willshire. 2005. "Iterative Rework: The Good, the Bad, and the Ugly." *IEEE Computer* 38(9): 34–41.

Gause, Donald C., and Brian Lawrence. 1999. "User-Driven Design." *Software Testing & Quality Engineering* 1(1): 22–28.

Gause, Donald C., and Gerald M. Weinberg. 1989. *Exploring Requirements: Quality Before Design*. New York: Dorset House Publishing.

Gilb, Tom. 2005. *Competitive Engineering: A Handbook for Systems Engineering, Requirements Engineering, and Software Engineering Using Planguage*. Oxford: Elsevier Butterworth-Heinemann.

Gilb, Tom, and Dorothy Graham. 1993. *Software Inspection*. Wokingham, UK: Addison-Wesley.

Goldstein, Harry. 2005. "Who Killed the Virtual Case File?" *IEEE Spectrum* 42(9): 24–35.

Grady, Robert B. 1999. "An Economic Release Decision Model: Insights into Software Project Management." In *Proceedings of the Applications of Software Measurement Conference*, 227–239. Orange Park, FL: Software Quality Engineering.

Hall, Tracy, Sara Beecham, and Austen Rainer. 2002. "Requirements Problems in Twelve Software Companies: An Empirical Analysis." *IEE Proceedings–Software*, 149(5): 153–60.

Hofmann, Hubert F., and Franz Lehner. 2001. "Requirements Engineering as a Success Factor in Software Projects." *IEEE Software* 18(4): 58–66.

Hooks, Ivy F., and Kristin A. Farry. 2001. *Customer-Centered Products: Creating Successful Products Through Smart Requirements Management.* New York: AMACOM.

Humphrey, Watts. 1998. "Your Date or Mine?" *news@sei* (September): Software Engineering Institute. *http://www.sei.cmu.edu/news-at-sei/columns/watts_new/1998/September/ watts-sep98.pdf.*

IEEE. 1990. IEEE Std. 610.12-1990: "IEEE Standard Glossary of Software Engineering Terminology." Los Alamitos, CA: IEEE Computer Society Press.

———. 1998. IEEE Std 830-1998: "IEEE Recommended Practice for Software Requirements Specifications." Los Alamitos, CA: IEEE Computer Society Press.

International Function Point Users Group (IFPUG). 2002. *Function Point Counting Practices Manual, Version 4.1.1.* Princeton Junction, NJ: International Function Point Users Group.

Jacobson, Ivar, Grady Booch, and James Rumbaugh. 1999. *The Unified Software Development Process.* Reading, MA: Addison-Wesley.

Jeffries, Ron, Ann Anderson, and Chet Hendrickson. 2001. *Extreme Programming Installed.* Boston: Addison-Wesley.

Jones, Capers. 2000. *Software Assessments, Benchmarks, and Best Practices.* Boston: Addison-Wesley.

Karner, Gustav. 1993. "Resource Estimation for Objectory Projects." *http://www.bfpug.com.br/ Artigos/UCP/Karner%20-%20Resource%20Estimation%20for%20Objectory%20Projects.doc.*

Kulak, Daryl, and Eamonn Guiney. 2004. *Use Cases: Requirements in Context, Second Edition.* Boston: Addison-Wesley.

Lauesen, Soren. 2002. *Software Requirements: Styles and Techniques.* London: Addison-Wesley.

Leffingwell, Dean. 1997. "Calculating the Return on Investment from More Effective Requirements Management." *American Programmer* 10(4): 13–16.

Leffingwell, Dean, and Don Widrig. 2003. *Managing Software Requirements, Second Edition: A Use Case Approach.* Boston: Addison-Wesley.

McConnell, Steve. 1998. *Software Project Survival Guide.* Redmond, WA: Microsoft Press.

———. 2006. *Software Estimation: Demystifying the Black Art.* Redmond, WA: Microsoft Press.

Morgan, Tony. 2002. *Business Rules and Information Systems: Aligning IT with Business Goals.* Boston: Addison-Wesley.

Nejmeh, Brian A., and Ian Thomas. 2002. "Business-Driven Product Planning Using Feature Vectors and Increments." *IEEE Software* 19(6): 34–42.

Ribu, Kirsten. 2001. "Estimating Object-Oriented Software Projects with Use Cases." Master of Science Thesis, University of Oslo. *http://bfpug.com.br/Artigos/UCP/Ribu-Estimating_O-O_SW_Projects_with_Use_Cases.pdf.*

Robertson, James. 2002. "Eureka! Why Analysts Should Invent Requirements." *IEEE Software* 19(4): 20–22.

Robertson, James, and Suzanne Robertson. 1994. *Complete Systems Analysis: The Workbook, The Textbook, The Answers.* New York: Dorset House Publishing.

Robertson, Suzanne, and James Robertson. 1999. *Mastering the Requirements Process.* Harlow, UK: Addison-Wesley.

Rodrigues, Alexandre. 2001. "Project Goals, Business Performance, and Risk." Cutter Consortium e-Project Management Advisory Service Executive Update 2(7).

Ross, Ronald G. 2003. *Principles of the Business Rule Approach.* Boston: Addison-Wesley.

Sheldon, F., et al. 1992. "Reliability Measurement from Theory to Practice." *IEEE Software* 9(4): 13–20.

Sommerville, Ian, and Pete Sawyer. 1997. *Requirements Engineering: A Good Practice Guide.* Chichester, UK: John Wiley & Sons.

The Standish Group. 2003. "What Are Your Requirements?" West Yarmouth, MA: The Standish Group International, Inc.

von Halle, Barbara. 2002. *Business Rules Applied: Building Better Systems Using the Business Rules Approach.* New York: John Wiley and Sons.

Whitmire, Scott A. 1995. "An Introduction to 3D Function Points." *Software Development,* 3(4): 43–53.

Wiegers, Karl E. 1996. *Creating a Software Engineering Culture.* New York: Dorset House Publishing.

——. 1999. "Software Process Improvement in Web Time." *IEEE Software* 15(4): 78–86.

——. 2000. "Stop Promising Miracles." *Software Development* 8(2): 49–54.

——. 2001. "Measuring Requirements Management: Getting to Know Your Requirements Data." *StickyMinds.com*, May 21, 2001.

——. 2002a. *Peer Reviews in Software: A Practical Guide.* Boston: Addison-Wesley.

———. 2002b. "Success Criteria Breed Success." *TheRationalEdge.com* (February). *http://www-128.ibm.com/developerworks/rational/library/2950.html.*

———. 2002c. "Saving for a Rainy Day." *TheRationalEdge.com* (April). *http://www-128.ibm.com/developerworks/rational/library/content/RationalEdge/apr02/RainyDayApr02.pdf.*

———. 2003a. *Software Requirements, Second Edition.* Redmond, WA: Microsoft Press.

———. 2003b. "See You in Court." *Software Development* 11(1): 36–40.

Wilson, Peter B. 1995. "Testable Requirements–An Alternative Sizing Measure." *The Journal of the Quality Assurance Institute* 9(4): 3–11.

Index

About the Author

Karl E. Wiegers is Principal Consultant with Process Impact, a software process consulting and education company in Portland, Oregon. His interests include requirements engineering, peer reviews, process improvement, project management, risk management, and software metrics. Previously, he spent 18 years at Eastman Kodak Company, where he held positions as a photographic research scientist, software developer, software manager, and software process and quality improvement leader. Karl received a B.S. degree in chemistry from Boise State College, and M.S. and Ph.D. degrees in organic chemistry from the University of Illinois. He is a member of the IEEE, IEEE Computer Society, and ACM.

Karl's most recent book is *More About Software Requirements: Thorny Issues and Practical Advice* (Microsoft Press, 2006). He also wrote *Software Requirements, Second Edition* (Microsoft Press, 2003), *Peer Reviews in Software: A Practical Guide* (Addison-Wesley, 2002), and *Creating a Software Engineering Culture* (Dorset House, 1996), as well as 160 articles on software development, chemistry, and military history. Karl is a two-time winner of the Productivity Award from *Software Development* magazine. Karl has served on the Editorial Board for *IEEE Software* magazine and as a contributing editor for *Software Development* magazine. He is a frequent speaker at software conferences and professional society meetings. In his spare time, Karl enjoys playing guitar, drinking wine, watching movies, and studying military history. You can reach him at *http://www.processimpact.com*.

Additional Resources for Visual Basic Developers

Published and Forthcoming Titles from Microsoft Press

Microsoft® Visual Basic® 2005 Express Edition: Build a Program Now!
Patrice Pelland ● ISBN 0-7356-2213-2

Featuring a full working edition of the software, this fun and highly visual guide walks you through a complete programming project—a desktop weather-reporting application—from start to finish. You'll get an introduction to the Microsoft Visual Studio® development environment and learn how to put the lightweight, easy-to-use tools in Visual Basic Express to work right away—creating, compiling, testing, and delivering your first ready-to-use program. You'll get expert tips, coaching, and visual examples each step of the way, along with pointers to additional learning resources.

Microsoft Visual Basic 2005 *Step by Step*
Michael Halvorson ● ISBN 0-7356-2131-4

With enhancements across its visual designers, code editor, language, and debugger that help accelerate the development and deployment of robust, elegant applications across the Web, a business group, or an enterprise, Visual Basic 2005 focuses on enabling developers to rapidly build applications. Now you can teach yourself the essentials of working with Visual Studio 2005 and the new features of the Visual Basic language—one step at a time. Each chapter puts you to work, showing you how, when, and why to use specific features of Visual Basic and guiding as you create actual components and working applications for Microsoft Windows®. You'll also explore data management and Web-based development topics.

Programming Microsoft Visual Basic 2005 *Core Reference*
Francesco Balena ● ISBN 0-7356-2183-7

Get the expert insights, indispensable reference, and practical instruction needed to exploit the core language features and capabilities in Visual Basic 2005. Well-known Visual Basic programming author Francesco Balena expertly guides you through the fundamentals, including modules, keywords, and inheritance, and builds your mastery of more advanced topics such as delegates, assemblies, and My Namespace. Combining in-depth reference with extensive, hands-on code examples and best-practices advice, this *Core Reference* delivers the key resources that you need to develop professional-level programming skills for smart clients and the Web.

Programming Microsoft Visual Basic 2005 Framework Reference
Francesco Balena ● ISBN 0-7356-2175-6

Complementing *Programming Microsoft Visual Basic 2005 Core Reference*, this book covers a wide range of additional topics and information critical to Visual Basic developers, including Windows Forms, working with Microsoft ADO.NET 2.0 and ASP.NET 2.0, Web services, security, remoting, and much more. Packed with sample code and real-world examples, this book will help developers move from understanding to mastery.

Programming Microsoft Windows Forms
Charles Petzold ● ISBN 0-7356-2153-5

Programming Microsoft Web Forms
Douglas J. Reilly ● ISBN 0-7356-2179-9

Debugging, Tuning, and Testing Microsoft .NET 2.0 Applications
John Robbins ● ISBN 0-7356-2202-7

Microsoft ASP.NET 2.0 *Step by Step*
George Shepherd ● ISBN 0-7356-2201-9

Microsoft ADO.NET 2.0 *Step by Step*
Rebecca Riordan ● ISBN 0-7356-2164-0

Programming Microsoft ASP.NET 2.0 *Core Reference*
Dino Esposito ● ISBN 0-7356-2176-4

For more information about Microsoft Press® books and other learning products,
visit: **www.microsoft.com/books** *and* **www.microsoft.com/learning**

Additional Resources for Web Developers

Published and Forthcoming Titles from Microsoft Press

Microsoft® Visual Web Developer™ 2005 Express Edition: Build a Web Site Now!
Jim Buyens • ISBN 0-7356-2212-4

With this lively, eye-opening, and hands-on book, all you need is a computer and the desire to learn how to create Web pages now using Visual Web Developer Express Edition! Featuring a full working edition of the software, this fun and highly visual guide walks you through a complete Web page project from set-up to launch. You'll get an introduction to the Microsoft Visual Studio® environment and learn how to put the light-weight, easy-to-use tools in Visual Web Developer Express to work right away—building your first, dynamic Web pages with Microsoft ASP.NET 2.0. You'll get expert tips, coaching, and visual examples at each step of the way, along with pointers to additional learning resources.

Microsoft ASP.NET 2.0 Programming
Step by Step
George Shepherd • ISBN 0-7356-2201-9

With dramatic improvements in performance, productivity, and security features, Visual Studio 2005 and ASP.NET 2.0 deliver a simplified, high-performance, and powerful Web development experience. ASP.NET 2.0 features a new set of controls and infrastructure that simplify Web-based data access and include functionality that facilitates code reuse, visual consistency, and aesthetic appeal. Now you can teach yourself the essentials of working with ASP.NET 2.0 in the Visual Studio environment— one step at a time. With *Step by Step*, you work at your own pace through hands-on, learn-by-doing exercises. Whether you're a beginning programmer or new to this version of the technology, you'll understand the core capabilities and fundamental techniques for ASP.NET 2.0. Each chapter puts you to work, showing you how, when, and why to use specific features of the ASP.NET 2.0 rapid application development environment and guiding you as you create actual components and working applications for the Web, including advanced features such as personalization.

Programming Microsoft ASP.NET 2.0
Core Reference
Dino Esposito • ISBN 0-7356-2176-4

Delve into the core topics for ASP.NET 2.0 programming, mastering the essential skills and capabilities needed to build high-performance Web applications successfully. Well-known ASP.NET author Dino Esposito deftly builds your expertise with Web forms, Visual Studio, core controls, master pages, data access, data binding, state management, security services, and other must-know topics—combining definitive reference with practical, hands-on programming instruction. Packed with expert guidance and pragmatic examples, this *Core Reference* delivers the key resources that you need to develop professional-level Web programming skills.

Programming Microsoft ASP.NET 2.0
Applications: *Advanced Topics*
Dino Esposito • ISBN 0-7356-2177-2

Master advanced topics in ASP.NET 2.0 programming—gaining the essential insights and in-depth understanding that you need to build sophisticated, highly functional Web applications successfully. Topics include Web forms, Visual Studio 2005, core controls, master pages, data access, data binding, state management, and security considerations. Developers often discover that the more they use ASP.NET, the more they need to know. With expert guidance from ASP.NET authority Dino Esposito, you get the in-depth, comprehensive information that leads to full mastery of the technology.

Programming Microsoft Windows® Forms
Charles Petzold • ISBN 0-7356-2153-5

Programming Microsoft Web Forms
Douglas J. Reilly • ISBN 0-7356-2179-9

CLR via C++
Jeffrey Richter with Stanley B. Lippman
ISBN 0-7356-2248-5

Debugging, Tuning, and Testing Microsoft .NET 2.0 Applications
John Robbins • ISBN 0-7356-2202-7

CLR via C#, Second Edition
Jeffrey Richter • ISBN 0-7356-2163-2

For more information about Microsoft Press® books and other learning products,
visit: **www.microsoft.com/books** *and* **www.microsoft.com/learning**

Additional Resources for C# Developers

Published and Forthcoming Titles from Microsoft Press

Microsoft® Visual C#® 2005 Express Edition: Build a Program Now!
Patrice Pelland • ISBN 0-7356-2229-9

In this lively, eye-opening, and hands-on book, all you need is a computer and the desire to learn how to program with Visual C# 2005 Express Edition. Featuring a full working edition of the software, this fun and highly visual guide walks you through a complete programming project—a desktop weather-reporting application—from start to finish. You'll get an unintimidating introduction to the Microsoft Visual Studio® development environment and learn how to put the lightweight, easy-to-use tools in Visual C# Express to work right away—creating, compiling, testing, and delivering your first, ready-to-use program. You'll get expert tips, coaching, and visual examples at each step of the way, along with pointers to additional learning resources.

Microsoft Visual C# 2005 *Step by Step*
John Sharp • ISBN 0-7356-2129-2

Visual C#, a feature of Visual Studio 2005, is a modern programming language designed to deliver a productive environment for creating business frameworks and reusable object-oriented components. Now you can teach yourself essential techniques with Visual C#—and start building components and Microsoft Windows®–based applications—one step at a time. With *Step by Step*, you work at your own pace through hands-on, learn-by-doing exercises. Whether you're a beginning programmer or new to this particular language, you'll learn how, when, and why to use specific features of Visual C# 2005. Each chapter puts you to work, building your knowledge of core capabilities and guiding you as you create your first C#-based applications for Windows, data management, and the Web.

Programming Microsoft Visual C# 2005 Framework Reference
Francesco Balena • ISBN 0-7356-2182-9

Complementing *Programming Microsoft Visual C# 2005 Core Reference*, this book covers a wide range of additional topics and information critical to Visual C# developers, including Windows Forms, working with Microsoft ADO.NET 2.0 and Microsoft ASP.NET 2.0, Web services, security, remoting, and much more. Packed with sample code and real-world examples, this book will help developers move from understanding to mastery.

Programming Microsoft Visual C# 2005 *Core Reference*
Donis Marshall • ISBN 0-7356-2181-0

Get the in-depth reference and pragmatic, real-world insights you need to exploit the enhanced language features and core capabilities in Visual C# 2005. Programming expert Donis Marshall deftly builds your proficiency with classes, structs, and other fundamentals, and advances your expertise with more advanced topics such as debugging, threading, and memory management. Combining incisive reference with hands-on coding examples and best practices, this *Core Reference* focuses on mastering the C# skills you need to build innovative solutions for smart clients and the Web.

CLR via C#, Second Edition
Jeffrey Richter • ISBN 0-7356-2163-2

In this new edition of Jeffrey Richter's popular book, you get focused, pragmatic guidance on how to exploit the common language runtime (CLR) functionality in Microsoft .NET Framework 2.0 for applications of all types—from Web Forms, Windows Forms, and Web services to solutions for Microsoft SQL Server™, Microsoft code names "Avalon" and "Indigo," consoles, Microsoft Windows NT® Service, and more. Targeted to advanced developers and software designers, this book takes you under the covers of .NET for an in-depth understanding of its structure, functions, and operational components, demonstrating the most practical ways to apply this knowledge to your own development efforts. You'll master fundamental design tenets for .NET and get hands-on insights for creating high-performance applications more easily and efficiently. The book features extensive code examples in Visual C# 2005.

Programming Microsoft Windows Forms
Charles Petzold • ISBN 0-7356-2153-5

CLR via C++
Jeffrey Richter with Stanley B. Lippman
ISBN 0-7356-2248-5

Programming Microsoft Web Forms
Douglas J. Reilly • ISBN 0-7356-2179-9

Debugging, Tuning, and Testing Microsoft .NET 2.0 Applications
John Robbins • ISBN 0-7356-2202-7

For more information about Microsoft Press® books and other learning products, visit: **www.microsoft.com/books** *and* **www.microsoft.com/learning**

Additional SQL Server Resources for Developers

Published and Forthcoming Titles from Microsoft Press

Microsoft® SQL Server™ 2005 Express Edition
Step by Step
Jackie Goldstein • ISBN 0-7356-2184-5

Teach yourself how to get database projects up and running
quickly with SQL Server Express
Edition—a free, easy-to-use
database product that is based
on SQL Server 2005 technology.
It's designed for building simple,
dynamic applications, with all
the rich functionality of the SQL
Server database engine and
using the same data access APIs,
such as Microsoft ADO.NET, SQL
Native Client, and T-SQL.
Whether you're new to database
programming or new to SQL Server, you'll learn how, when, and
why to use specific features of this simple but powerful database development environment. Each chapter puts you to work,
building your knowledge of core capabilities and guiding you
as you create actual components and working applications.

Microsoft SQL Server 2005 Programming
Step by Step
Fernando Guerrero • ISBN 0-7356-2207-8

SQL Server 2005 is Microsoft's
next-generation data management and analysis solution that
delivers enhanced scalability,
availability, and security features
to enterprise data and analytical
applications while making them
easier to create, deploy, and
manage. Now you can teach
yourself how to design, build, test,
deploy, and maintain SQL Server
databases—one step at a time.
Instead of merely focusing on
describing new features, this book shows new database
programmers and administrators how to use specific features
within typical business scenarios. Each chapter provides a highly
practical learning experience that demonstrates how to build
database solutions to solve common business problems.

Microsoft SQL Server 2005 Analysis Services
Step by Step
Hitachi Consulting Services • ISBN 0-7356-2199-3

One of the key features of SQL Server 2005 is SQL Server Analysis
Services—Microsoft's customizable analysis solution for business
data modeling and interpretation. Just compare SQL Server
Analysis Services to its competition to understand the great
value of its enhanced features. One of the keys to harnessing
the full functionality of SQL Server will be leveraging Analysis
Services for the powerful tool that it is—including creating a cube,
and deploying, customizing, and extending the basic calculations. This step-by-step tutorial discusses how to get started, how
to build scalable analytical applications, and how to use and ad-
minister advanced features. Interactivity (enhanced in SQL Server
2005), data translation, and security are also covered in detail.

Microsoft SQL Server 2005 Reporting Services
Step by Step
Hitachi Consulting Services • ISBN 0-7356-2250-7

SQL Server Reporting Services (SRS) is Microsoft's customizable
reporting solution for business data analysis. It is one of the key
value features of SQL Server 2005: functionality more advanced
and much less expensive than its competition. SRS is powerful,
so an understanding of how to architect a report, as well as how
to install and program SRS, is key to harnessing the full functionality of SQL Server. This procedural tutorial shows how to use the
Report Project Wizard, how to think about and access data, and
how to build queries. It also walks through the creation of charts
and visual layouts for maximum visual understanding of data
analysis. Interactivity (enhanced in SQL Server 2005) and security
are also covered in detail.

Programming Microsoft SQL Server 2005
Andrew J. Brust, Stephen Forte, and William H. Zack
ISBN 0-7356-1923-9

This thorough, hands-on reference for developers and database
administrators teaches the basics of programming custom applications with SQL Server 2005. You will learn the fundamentals
of creating database applications—including coverage of
T-SQL, Microsoft .NET Framework, and Microsoft ADO.NET. In
addition to practical guidance on database architecture and
design, application development, and reporting and data
analysis, this essential reference guide covers performance,
tuning, and availability of SQL Server 2005.

Inside Microsoft SQL Server 2005:
The Storage Engine
Kalen Delaney • ISBN 0-7356-2105-5

Inside Microsoft SQL Server 2005:
T-SQL Programming
Itzik Ben-Gan • ISBN 0-7356-2197-7

Inside Microsoft SQL Server 2005:
Query Processing and Optimization
Kalen Delaney • ISBN 0-7356-2196-9

Programming Microsoft ADO.NET 2.0 Core Reference
David Sceppa • ISBN 0-7356-2206-X

For more information about Microsoft Press® books and other learning products,
visit: **www.microsoft.com/mspress** *and* **www.microsoft.com/learning**

What do you think of this book? We want to hear from you!

Do you have a few minutes to participate in a brief online survey? Microsoft is interested in hearing your feedback about this publication so that we can continually improve our books and learning resources for you.

To participate in our survey, please visit:

www.microsoft.com/learning/booksurvey

And enter this book's ISBN, 0-7356-2267-1. As a thank-you to survey participants in the United States and Canada, each month we'll randomly select five respondents to win one of five $100 gift certificates from a leading online merchant.* At the conclusion of the survey, you can enter the drawing by providing your e-mail address, which will be used for prize notification *only*.

Thanks in advance for your input. Your opinion counts!

Sincerely,

Microsoft Learning

Microsoft | Learning

Learn More. Go Further.